A History of
WORCESTERSHIRE

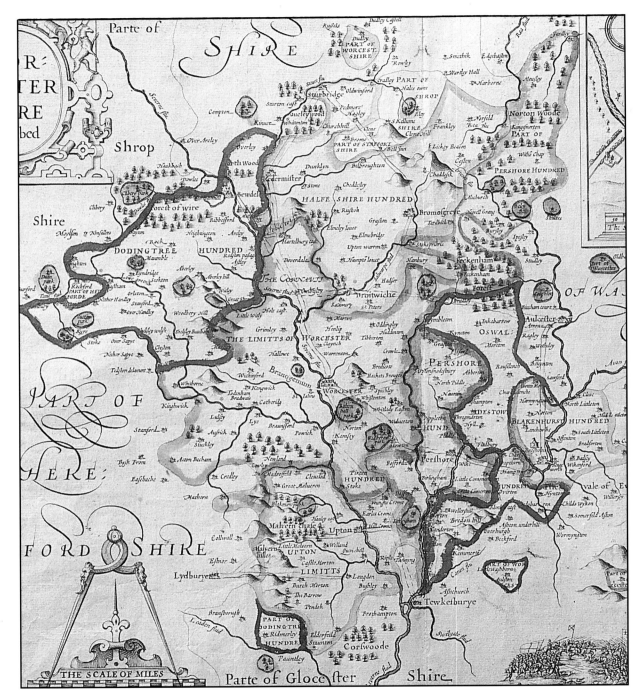

John Speed's map of Worcestershire, 1610

**THE DARWEN COUNTY
HISTORY SERIES**

A History of
WORCESTERSHIRE

David Lloyd

**Cartography by David Bilbey
Marginal illustrations by Jean Lissauer**

Phillimore

First published 1993
Reprinted 2002

Published by
PHILLIMORE & CO. LTD
Shopwyke Manor Barn, Chichester, West Sussex

ISBN 0 85033 658 9

Printed and bound in Great Britain by
BUTLER & TANNER LTD
London and Frome

Contents

List of Illustrations

Frontispiece : Speed's map of 1610

Colour Plates

Acknowledgements

Very special thanks must go to David Bilbey for the cartography for all of the maps and plans; and to Jean Lissauer for the marginal illustrations.

Grateful thanks must also go to the following for their co-operation and permission to reproduce the following illustrations:

Bewdley Town Council, 86; Birmingham Museum and Art Gallery, 121, plate XII; British Railways, Central Photographic Board (Derek Harrison), 107; Cambridge University, Director of Aerial Photography, 31; Dudley Public Libraries Services, 90, 111, 112; Elfincolour, 51, 65; Lamplight Research and Lighting (Alison M. Doggett and Leslie W. Hepple), 30, 87, 129, 131; plates II, III, IV, V, X, XVI; Malvern Museums, 50, 106; Royal Commission on the Historical Monuments of England (Avoncroft), 52; Royal Commission on the Historical Monuments of England (W. A. Barker), 13, 14, 17, 100; Gareth Thomas, F.R.P.S., plates VII, VIII, IX, XIII, XIV, XV; Warwickshire and Worcestershire Life, plate I; Weidenfeld (Publishers) Ltd., 118, 119; Wyre Forest District Museums Service, plate VI.

The following illustrations were supplied by the author; 19-21, 33, 34, 39-44, 73, 91-95, 130, 132, plate XI.

Preface

I am not a native of Worcestershire but I have known it well for most of my life. As a child, I was born and brought up at Ludlow, only a few miles beyond the county boundary. As an adult, before moving back to Ludlow, I lived in Yardley, now a suburb of Birmingham but until 1909 the north-east corner of Worcestershire.

My association with Worcestershire began in 1948, when I saw Bradman score a century at the county cricket ground at the start of the Australian tour, an experience I shall always savour. In later years I was a keen cyclist, and spent happy hours exploring lanes of the Teme valley, in among the hop fields. As parents in Birmingham in the 1960s and 1970s, my wife and I often took our young family up on to the Clent and Lickey Hills, and sometimes further afield, for walks on the Malverns or Bredon Hill.

My interest in the history of the county goes back to the late 1970s, when I began to take adult classes in local and architectural history for what was then the Extra-Mural Department of Birmingham University. These classes took me for many years to Bewdley and for a shorter period to Chaddesley Corbett, while a thriving research class at Bromsgrove still meets regularly at the Methodist Centre on Monday mornings. In addition, I have given talks at various times in Droitwich, Kidderminster, Malvern, Upton-on-Severn and Worcester, and have thus met a number of people up and down the county who are keenly interested in its history.

Tutoring in adult education, like the best teaching everywhere, is not simply the imparting of knowledge. It is the organisation of a learning experience for a group of people, often of widely differing backgrounds, experiences and expertise. The dedication of this book to the members of two of those classes is a small acknowledgement of what I have learnt from them, and of the insights into the history of Worcestershire which we worked out together.

I am grateful to many people who have helped with the preparation of this book, but my special thanks go to my wife, Wendy. She has accompanied me on various expeditions into Worcestershire, waiting without complaint as I burrowed in libraries or explored remote churchyards.

This book is dedicated

to the members of the Historical Research Groups

at Bewdley and Bromsgrove

Introduction

Worcestershire's Historians and Writers

The known tradition of Worcestershire history begins with Florence of Worcester (d.1118), a monk of St Mary's Priory, Worcester, who edited a number of Anglo-Saxon chronicles, and wrote his own account of contemporary events. His concerns were national rather than local, but even before the 19th century Worcestershire had two major county histories, both written by members of the land-owning, gentry class.

The first was Thomas Habington (1560-1647) of Hindlip, a political activist who was involved in the Gunpowder Plot of 1605. He was pardoned but only on condition that he never again left Worcestershire. He spent the last 40 years of his life travelling round the county, copying epitaphs, delving into genealogy and setting it all down in fat volumes which were published in 1717 and 1723.

His successor was the Rev. Treadway Russell Nash, D. D. (1725-1811), Vicar of Warndon and later of St Peter's, Droitwich. He was a magistrate and a classical scholar but spent most of his time compiling his collections for *The History of Worcestershire*, published between 1781 and 1799. He was able to complete this, he maintained, 'by eschewing elections, gaming, horse racing, fox hunting and other pleasures as are too frequently the ruin of country gentlemen'.

Many of the great topographical writers and diarists visited Worcestershire, including John Leland, Celia Fiennes, Daniel Defoe, Lord Byng (author of *The Torrington Diaries*) and William Cobbett. The county has been well served with trade directories and early newspapers. For the historian, however, the greatest blessings are the fine volumes of the Worcestershire Record Society, which make available such important source material as the 1275 lay subsidy or the court rolls of the Manor of Hales. The volumes of the *Victoria County History*, published between 1901 and 1924, and the *Transactions of the Worcestershire Archaeological Society*, published from 1923, are other important sources. The Worcestershire Record Office, now divided between the medieval St Helen's church in the centre of Worcester and lavish new quarters at County Hall, makes a wide range of other documents readily available to researchers. The county has a wealth of good libraries and museums, including the County Museum in the magnificent setting of the Bishop's Palace at Hartlebury Castle and a Civil War centre in Worcester's medieval Commandery.

Many novelists and poets give glimpses of Worcestershire life. The most remarkable is William Langland (*c*.1330-*c*.1400), who was born in or near the county, and was probably educated at Great Malvern Priory. His *Vision concerning*

1 *Thomas Habington (1560-1647), as portrayed in Nash's Worcestershire*

2 *Treadway Russell Nash, D.D. (1725-1811)*

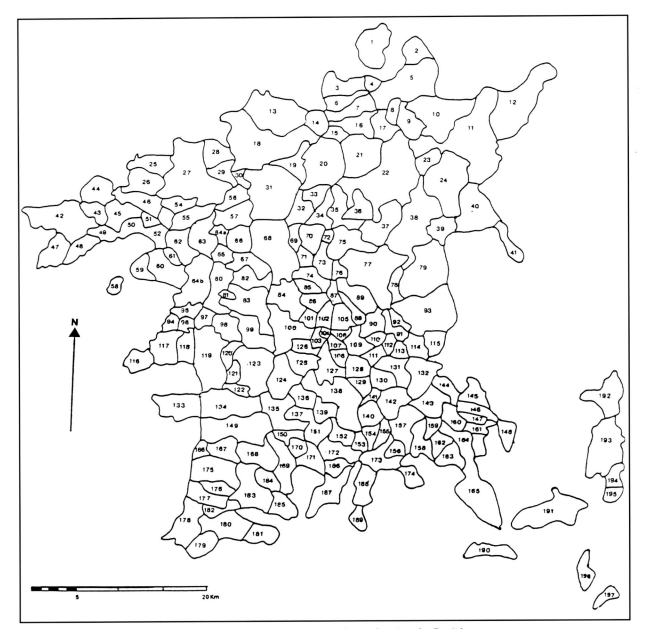

3 *The historic County of Worcestershire, showing the Parishes*

The Parishes

Piers the Plowman, though written in London, gives a picture of rural life which was almost certainly inspired by Worcestershire. Francis Brett Young (1884-1954), writing about the industrial Midlands, and John Moore (1907-1967), writing about the villages around Bredon Hill, are other truly regional writers.

A number of modern poets refer to Worcestershire, but most references are tantalisingly brief, for example John Drinkwater (1882-1937), '... never went to Mamble, That lies above the Teme'. Even the best known, A. E. Housman (1859-1936), who was born in Bromsgrove and whose statue now stands in Bromsgrove High Street, wrote very sparingly about his native county, though his melancholy and emotive verses on Bredon Hill are among his most memorable works:

> But when the snows at Christmas
> On Bredon top were strown,
> My love rose up so early
> And stole out unbeknown
> And went to church alone.
>
> They tolled the one bell only,
> Groom there was none to see,
> The mourners follow'd after
> And so to church went she,
> And would not wait for me.

Yet the art form which best catches the quintessence of Worcestershire is probably music, through the compositions of Edward Elgar (1857-1934), Housman's near contemporary. Now rated the first great English composer since Purcell, Elgar spent nearly all his creative years within sight of the Malvern Hills. 'No one was more imbued with his own countryside', said Elgar's daughter, 'than my father.' 'If ever you're walking on the hills', Elgar is reputed to have said of his Cello Concerto 'and hear this, don't be frightened, it's only me!'

Chapter 1

The Size and Shape of Worcestershire, and its Physical Features

Worcestershire is one of the smaller counties of England. Before the merger with Herefordshire in 1974 it was 33rd in size of the 41 counties. It was only an eighth of the area of Yorkshire, a quarter that of Lincolnshire and not quite as large as each of its neighbours: Herefordshire to the west, Gloucestershire to the south, Warwickshire to the east, Staffordshire to the north and Shropshire to the north-west.

Measured by population, Worcestershire ranked a little higher than it did by area. In 1801, the year of the first national census, the county had a population of 146,000, the 21st largest in England. It had more people than Herefordshire, though less than each of its other neighbours. By 1951, the population had risen to 523,000, but its rank order had dropped to 24th.

Worcestershire is generally considered to be part of the English Midlands. The county town is roughly equidistant from London, Exeter, Holyhead and York. For many administrative purposes Worcestershire is grouped with other Midland counties, as in the Heart of England Tourist Board. Yet it also has something of the air of the west country. The Hwicce, who settled the county in the sixth and seventh centuries, came up the Severn valley from the south-west, while in later periods the River Severn took much of the county's trade to Bristol. There are also historic links with Wales. The north-west of the county is only 15 miles from the Welsh border, and in the 16th and early 17th century Worcestershire was one of the border counties that were administered jointly with the Principality.

In the Middle Ages, Worcestershire was transitional between the richer south-east and the poorer north-west. Assessments of lay and clerical wealth show it as only the 30th county in 1334, though it was relatively richer by 1514. After 1600, particularly, Worcestershire benefited from the use made of the Severn as a busy commercial routeway while parts of the county had the resources for great industrial development. In the 19th century the north-east was part of the Black Country conurbation, a grim contrast to rural Worcestershire, which for many seemed the very heart of the English countryside. The M5 has now replaced the Severn as the major north to south routeway through the county and each day thousands who drive along it have glimpses of well-known landmarks like Bredon Hill, the Malverns or the tower of Worcester Cathedral.

100 miles

4 *Map of England and Wales, showing the position of Worcestershire*

E *Exeter*
H *Holyhead*
L *London*
Y *York*

and the distribution of wealth in England and Wales in 1334

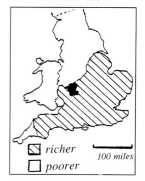

richer
poorer   *100 miles*

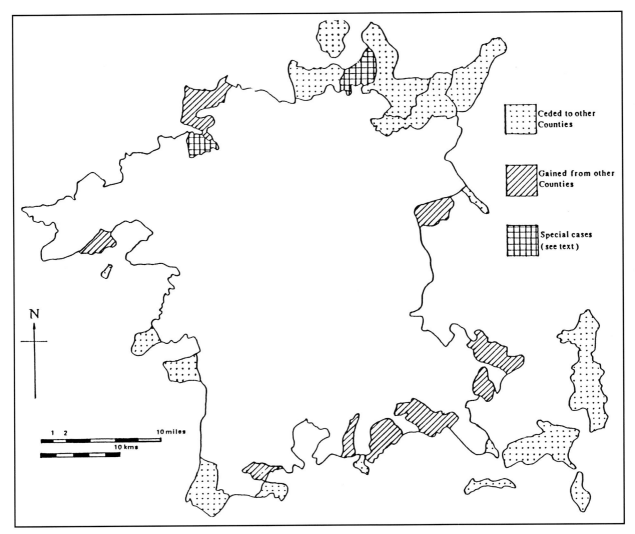

5 *The changing shape of Worcestershire, showing parishes ceded, parishes gained and 'special case' parishes*

Legend:
- Ceded to other Counties
- Gained from other Counties
- Special cases (see text)

N

1 2   10 miles
10 kms

The County Boundary

Few counties have experienced so many boundary changes as Worcestershire. Like Staffordshire and Warwickshire, the county was created in 918 as an administrative and defensive unit to resist the threat of Danish conquest from the east. The new boundary took account of the huge estates already held by the Bishop of Worcester and the great religious houses, many of which formed detached blocks to the south and east. One such block, some six miles east of the present county boundary, consisted of the parishes of Shipston-on-Stour and Tredington, which were held by the bishop, and Alderminster, of Pershore Abbey. Blockley, Cutsdean, Evenlode and Daylesford were other detached parishes to the south-east, as was Dudley in the north. The main body of the county itself had many protruding spurs, like the narrow parish of Oldberrow which reached south-eastwards into Warwickshire from Beoley, or the more solid shape of Mathon to the west, driving a wedge into Herefordshire. Neighbouring counties drove their own spurs into Worcestershire, while from the end of the 11th century until 1844 part of Halesowen was an enigmatic outlier of Shropshire, due to ownership of the manor by the powerful Earl of Shrewsbury, who annexed it to his county of residence. The greatest anomaly was Bewdley, which became a sanctuary for criminals in the late Middle Ages because of uncertainty whether it belonged to Worcestershire or Shropshire. Incidents such as that of Thomas Tye, priest, who 'preached sedition, but the justices being here in the shire ground could not proceed', finally led to an Act of Parliament in 1544, which settled for Worcestershire.

There were no further adjustments until 1844, when a number of changes followed the Reform Act of 1832. Further rationalisation took place in the 1890s, after the new county councils had been established in 1889, but the most sweeping changes did not occur until the 20th century. These began with the transfer of the north-east spur of the county—Yardley, Northfield and most of King's Norton—to the City of Birmingham, the suburbs of which had been creeping outwards since the early 19th century, especially after the coming of the railways. There were further changes in the 1920s. The ragged edge along the south of the county was straightened when six parishes between Bredon and Broadway were absorbed into Worcestershire. In compensation, two parishes in the extreme south-west were ceded to Gloucestershire. All the outlying blocks were also transferred to other authorities, including Dudley, which became a county borough in 1929.

6 *St Egburgha's church and the Old Grammar School, Yardley, which was ceded to Birmingham in 1911*

The last and most radical changes occurred in 1974, as part of a wide sweeping Local Government Act. There were adjustments in the north, where Halesowen and Stourbridge were absorbed into the new West Midlands Metropolitan District. At the same time, Worcestershire and Herefordshire were amalgamated to create the new county of Hereford and Worcester. This was divided up into a number of new administrative districts, two of which, Leominster and Malvern Hills, absorbed parts of both former counties. A map of the post-1974 administrative districts is shown on p.118, as part of Chapter 10.

These boundary changes pose problems for the historian. This book concentrates on the county as it was immediately before 1974, but some reference is also made to former parts of the county, particularly to Dudley, which was the second largest town in Worcestershire for most of the 19th century. The frequent alterations of area do mean, however, that statistical comparisons are rarely precise, and that distributional maps may have to be approximated near the county boundaries.

Topography and Drainage

Worcestershire has been compared to a shallow basin, surrounded by an indented rim of upland. The central part of the county, sometimes called the plain of Worcestershire, is an undulating lowland on either side of the Severn. This merges south-eastwards with the lower Avon valley, commonly called the Vale of Evesham and long known for its fertility. In 1585 the antiquarian William Camden in his *Britannia* wrote that this region '... well deserved to be called the Granary of All these counties, so good and plentiful is the grounde in yieldinge the best corn abundantly ... '. Near the confluence of the two rivers the land drops to under 10 metres, but much of the lowland is between 20 and 60 metres high, with occasional knolls standing above it. It rises to low hills to the east of the Severn in the far north of the county.

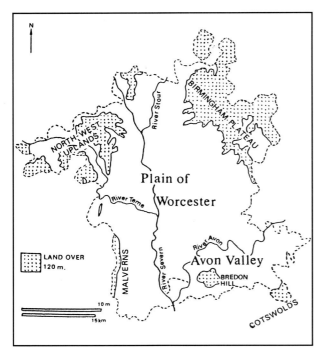

7a *The main physical features of Worcestershire*

7b *The drainage network of Worcestershire*

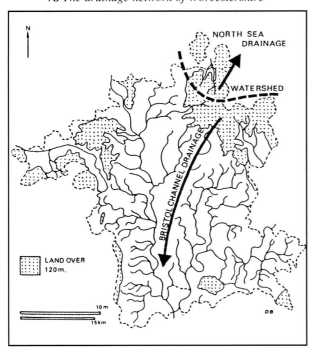

The north-west uplands, stretching to the county border, are a dissected upland, much of which lies between 120 and 200 metres. The Severn and the Teme divide this up into blocks which have their own local names such as the Kyre Uplands or Wyre Forest. Blackstone and Redstone Rocks, both with caves used as hermitages until the 19th century, are among several scenic features along the Severn valley, while the historian Habington 'noted the bountifil dowre of fruytfull ground' lying along the Teme.

The north-east uplands are part of the Birmingham plateau, which culminates in the Clents and the Lickeys, both about 984 ft. high. These are now public amenity areas and have been nicknamed 'the playground of Birmingham'. In the Middle Ages the plateau was poorly developed but during the Industrial Revolution of the 18th and 19th centuries it became the most densely populated part of Worcestershire. Access to the plateau from the lowlands was then a problem, overcome by engineering feats like the 30-lock staircase at Tardebigge.

To the south-west the Malverns form a long, whale-backed ridge rising to 1,404 ft. at the Worcestershire Beacon. John Leland, passing here in 1540, put it succinctly when he wrote: 'Malverne hills ly a greate way in lengthe from southe to northe ...'. The range continues northwards to the Abberley Hills, marked by the very high clock tower which was added to Abberley Hall in 1883.

From the Malverns there are extensive views across the Severn and Avon valleys to the scarp edge of the Cotswolds. These are only inside the county boundary in the far south-east, where a salient pushing into Gloucestershire takes in Broadway Hill at just over 300 metres. The summit is crowned by Broadway Tower, a folly built in 1800 by Lord Coventry, allegedly so that his wife 'could enjoy the view'.

Bredon Hill, an outlier of the Cotswolds, attains almost the same height a few miles to the west. Its steep rise from the plain makes Bredon a well-known landmark. The poet A. E. Housman, however sombre his themes, caught the mood of rural Worcestershire when he wrote of Bredon Hill:

'Here of a Sunday morning, My love and I would lie, And see the coloured counties, And hear the larks so high, Above us in the sky'.

The River Severn gives Worcestershire a cohesion which is rare among English counties. Except for the far north-east, which now belongs to Birmingham and which ultimately drains into the North Sea, every part of the county is in the Severn basin. The Severn itself, its principal tributaries the Avon, the Stour and the Teme, and the smaller streams that drain into them, form a dendritic pattern which covers almost the whole county. This means that all rain falling on the county eventually flows with the Severn into the Bristol Channel, unless it is first evaporated or sinks underground. Until the advent of steam and motor transport the Severn and its major tributaries were the commercial arteries of Worcestershire. For part of its length, the Severn valley is still followed by the M5, the main commercial highway of today, but north of Worcester it climbs almost unnoticed on to the Birmingham plateau, with a disregard of physical restraints that would have been the envy of earlier generations.

Geology

The oldest parts of Worcestershire are the uplands of the north and west. These form the rim of a great amphitheatre, across which the solid geology gets progressively younger, until the newest strata in the county are encountered at Bredon Hill and in the Cotswolds. In many places, however, the landscape resulting from these underlying rocks has been modified by comparatively recent surface deposits, laid down by the Ice Sheets, by interglacial floods of meltwater or by rivers.

The old rocks forming the upland rim are of many kinds and ages. The oldest are the pre-Cambrian and Cambrian rocks of the Malverns and the Lickeys. Some of these are more than 600 million years old and have no fossils in them, because they predate the first known forms of life. The Malvernian rocks have been so metamorphosed by heat and pressure that their original character is unrecognisable. The faults and fractures which have left the Malverns as an inclined slice of hard rocks resistant to erosion continue northwards and rather younger rocks, formed in the deep seas of Silurian times, have been thrown up to form the Abberley Hills. To the west, Devonian Old Red Sandstone rocks form the hills of north-west Worcestershire.

The next geological period was the Carboniferous, when the area which is now north Worcestershire was a fluctuating border zone between upland to the south and lowland or sea to the north. These conditions caused layers of sandstones and shales while iron carried in solution from the land surfaces was precipitated in deltas to form ironstone. The climate was equatorial and at times luxuriant rain forests thrived, to be turned later into coal as the rotting vegetation was buried under mud and sand. These now outcrop in the Forest of Wyre, where the coal deposits are sparse, but also on the Midland plateau, where they form a southern continuation of the South Staffordshire coalfield. Metal industries first developed here because iron ore, timber for charcoal and limestone for a flux were all available, whereas conditions for farming were not good; but the availability of coal made this area a pace-setter of the Industrial Revolution.

8 A generalised block diagram of the Malverns. The arrow shows the main direction of the force which folded the ancient rocks

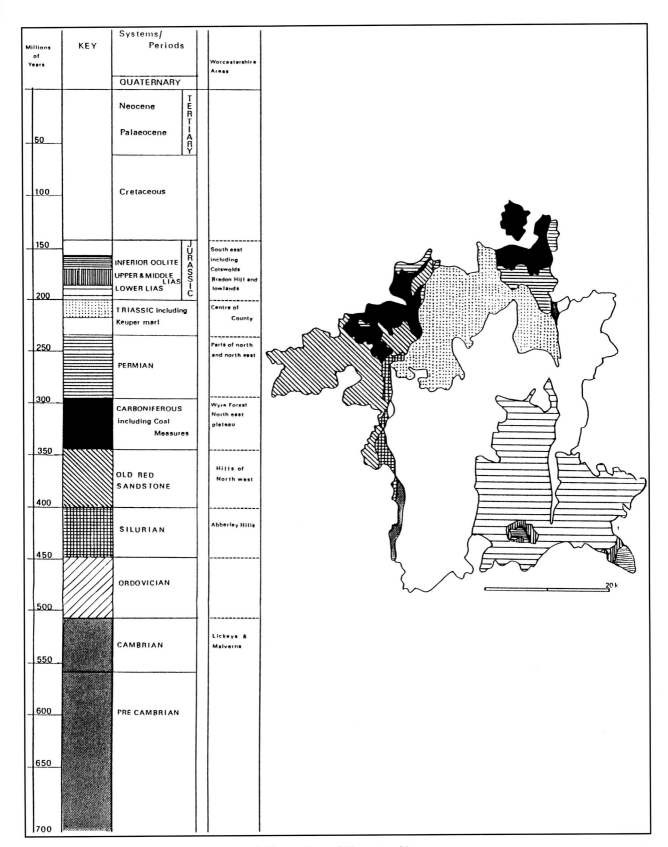

9 *The geology of Worcestershire*

Great earth movements now raised up the Pennines to the north and another upland to the east, while to the west the Welsh Highlands were already in existence. In Permian and Triassic times, there was a great basin between these uplands, from perhaps 270 to 180 million years ago. Britain was only a few hundred miles north of what was then the equator, and formed part of a great Sahara-like desert which stretched over much of north-west Europe. Sands and pebbles accumulated and also fine, wind-borne deposits known as loess. The thin coating of iron oxide which formed around each grain has given its characteristic redness to central Worcestershire. This redness shows in the county's ploughed fields, in its red sandstone churches and in its red bricks baked from Keuper marl. Intense solar evaporation from inland lakes also caused the salt deposits which are interbedded with the Triassic sandstones and marls in the Droitwich area.

South-eastwards, the Triassic rocks give way to the lower layers of the next major geological period, the Jurassic. Much of the Avon valley is covered by the Lower Lias, a bluish-grey clay interbedded with muddy limestones, and rich in ammonites and other fossils. The clay reflects the shallow sea which began to invade the desert at the end of Triassic times. Changing conditions led to a succession of sands, marlstones and clays, culminating in the Oolitic limestone which forms the capping of the Cotswolds and its outlier Bredon Hill. This is the well known honey-coloured Cotswold stone, which is a popular building material in south-east Worcestershire.

The rocks formed in this way were gently tilted, and then eroded over a great span of time, to form the essential fabric of the present landscape. But much of the detail was moulded during the glacial and interglacial periods of the last million years. During the early glaciations, great lakes were formed between advancing ice sheets and some of the uplands, and later overflowing caused new river channels to be adopted. The present courses of the Avon and the Severn were determined in this way. During interglacial periods, great floods of meltwater filled the valleys with thousands of tons of sands and gravels, out of which the rivers later cut wide, almost flat terraces, such as the 85-ft. terrace on which much of central Worcester is situated.

10 *An artists sketch of Palaeolithic men hunting mammoth on the edge of the ice sheets*

Climate and Vegetation

The cold, dry tundra conditions of the last Ice Age eventually gave way to warmer conditions, with the birch rapidly colonising much of Britain. A more continental Boreal period followed from about 7600 B.C. with oak and elm spreading from the continent across the land bridge which then existed. About 5500 B.C. this was succeeded by the milder, oceanic period of the Atlantic period, which added alder, ash, beech and lime. By about 3000 B.C. mixed woodland was established over most of Worcestershire, and this is still the theoretical climax vegetation of today, that is the vegetation which would reassert itself should all human management be withdrawn. Much of this indigenous growth was still standing in Anglo-Saxon times, when 24 different species were recorded in boundary charters, the most common references being to thorn (60), oak (43) and ash (24).

The climate, like so much else in Worcestershire, is transitional, between the drier, more extreme climate of the south-east and the wetter, moderate climate of

11 *A Palaeolithic hunter, using a stone tipped spear*

the west. As everywhere in Britain, air masses come from all directions, bringing different types of conditions, but in winter warm Atlantic air is often funnelled between the hills on either side of the Bristol channel, creating mild conditions in the Severn and Avon valleys. This creates what is sometimes called 'a gulf of winter warmth' in the Vale of Evesham, lessening the risk of spring frosts and encouraging the growth of fruit and early vegetables.

Two-thirds of Worcestershire is now agricultural land, won by man through centuries of laborious clearance and burning. Small areas of natural forest survive in among the extensive Forestry Commission plantations in Wyre Forest. Oak and birch are the dominant trees, but rarer specimens like the small-leaved lime are also present. Hazel dominates the undergrowth, much of it formerly coppiced, that is planted with closely set trees which were cut before fully grown for charcoal, wood fuel and lathes. In 1670 the local entrepreneur, Andrew Yarranton, was complaining that there were 'ten thousand acres of coppice in Wyre', so that 'there is not growing at this present, one hundred tun of good timber for ship-building'.

Heathland, moor and other woodland survive at high altitudes, as on the Clents and Lickeys, or on small patches of infertile soil. One of the best known is Hartlebury Common, sited on blown sand and old river gravel. This is a rich habitat for flora and fauna and is now preserved as a Local Nature Reserve. Remnants of more extensive uncultivated areas survive here and there in the county, as at Castlemorton Common, the last surviving relic of the former Malvern Chase, once a great hunting preserve between the Malverns and the River Severn.

Chapter 2

Prehistoric and Roman Worcestershire, before A.D.410

The Old and Middle Stone Age

The earliest human inhabitants of Worcestershire were primitive hunters and food gatherers, who moved about the area during the last phases of the third Ice Age. They used simple stone tools, examples of which have been found near Worcester and in the Stour valley. These tools have caused this long, remote period to be called the Palaeolithic or Old Stone Age. In some parts of the country traces of Palaeolithic man's existence have been found in caves but there is no such evidence in Worcestershire.

Between 7500 and 3000 B.C., as the climate improved and mixed woodland established itself over most of the country, men developed a slightly more advanced culture, known as the Mesolithic or Middle Stone Age. They made microliths, small edged flints which were mainly used to barb and top the arrows which they needed for hunting. Such microliths have been found in several places in the county, such as Baginton on Hartlebury Common, where light, easily worked soils had formed on the gravel terraces. These people were semi-nomadic, shifting their homes from site to site, probably cultivating small areas as well as hunting and fishing.

12 *Casting metal in the Bronze Age*

The New Stone Age

In the third millennium B.C., that is after the year 3000, men achieved a more advanced culture which is known as the Neolithic or New Stone Age. More effective stone tools were now made, and bone and wood were also used. Communities became more settled, and large tracts of land were cleared for cultivation and pasture around permanent villages. Local clays were used to make pottery and the dead were buried in elongated earth mounds known as long barrows. Over the last 30 years, aerial photography and intense field work have revealed that prehistoric settlement of this kind was much more extensive than had previously been thought, especially on the gravel terraces of the Rivers Avon and Severn. Large tracts of the primeval forest must have been cleared for cultivation and for pasture. So great are the postulated changes that some archaeologists have called this period the first agricultural revolution.

Major finds probably dating from this period include four cursus sites, all in the Avon valley. A cursus was a long, rectangular, ditched enclosure, probably

13 Conderton Camp on Bredon Hill. An elongated earthwork occupying a steep-sided spur with strong natural defences. The first earthwork dates from the second century B.C. but in the first century this was reduced in size. Circular huts with stone footings and storage pits have been found inside the smaller enclosure

associated with burial rites. One such site is at Netherton, south-west of Evesham, where there is a complex of crop marks and overlapping rectangular enclosures. At Nafford, in the parish of Eckington, a few miles to the west, aerial photography has revealed a number of ditched enclosures, and also a large, double-ditched circle. This is interpreted as a henge, that is a religious site which once had upstanding stones like those surviving in other parts of the country.

Finds in different parts of the county fill in some of the details of life in Neolithic Worcestershire. Ground and polished stone axes have been found at more than 20 sites, seven of them in the north-east, eight in the Severn valley, another six in the Avon valley and the south-east. The type of stone shows that some of these come from outside the county, indicating widespread trading activity with places as far away as Cornwall and Westmorland. In some cases, however, flint was imported into the county and then worked into axes on knapping floors, as at Tardebigge, where material has been picked up from four adjacent fields. Crude Neolithic pottery has been found near Broadway, where long barrows and ancient earthworks occur near the Gloucestershire border. The style of this and other pottery found in the Midlands resembles that of a large camp at Windmill Hill in Wiltshire and has caused some archaeologists to claim that the culture of the Neolithic Midlands is essentially that of southern England.

The Bronze Age

In the second millennium B.C., perhaps after 1700, men discovered bronze, an alloy made from copper and tin. This enabled them to make metal tools which were more efficient than stone. Bronze axes, spears and swords have been found at some 30 sites in Worcestershire, 18 of them in the Severn valley. Barbed and tanged arrowheads, on the other hand, have been found in greatest numbers in the Bredon Hill area.

Again, it is aerial photography which has made the most spectacular discoveries. Many small circular crop marks or 'ring ditches' have been found, some of which have been proved by excavation to represent ploughed-out Bronze Age round barrows. Bronze Age people disposed of their dead by cremation, after which the charred bones were placed in an urn or vessel which was buried in the barrow or mound. At Clent Heath and at Holt, concentrations of such features have been interpreted as large cemeteries. The former site, which has been known for a long time, once had five barrows, but now only two survive, both almost levelled by ploughing. This site was plundered by Bishop Lyttelton, an early antiquarian, in the 18th century, when he recovered three cremations and an urn.

The Iron Age

During the sixth and seventh centuries, iron tools and weapons began to be used, causing the last half millennium B.C. to be known as the Iron Age. People seem to have lived in small villages, like that recently excavated at Beckford, south-west of Evesham and almost on the county boundary. Here were a number of ditched enclosures, each full of buildings, including round houses and granaries. The houses were made of a circle of wooden poles with low wattle and daub walls and a thatched roof. There were a number of pits, used for storing grain and burning rubbish. The farms were surrounded by a ditch, probably with a fence of some kind, and there were small enclosed fields beyond. Elsewhere, however, traces of oblong buildings have been found.

There is no means of knowing what the balance was between arable and pastoral farming. Querns, primitive stone hand mills for grinding corn, have been

14 The marks of a 'henge' religous site at Nafford in the parish of Eckington, on a terrace of the River Avon. There may have been upstanding stones here, in two concentric circles. The henge probably dates from the third millennium B.C.

15 *Herefordshire Beacon, an impressive hill fort in the Malverns*

found at Badsey in the Avon valley. Some grain was kept in storage pits in the ground but four post granaries have been found in the Malverns. Animal bones are seldom well preserved in Worcestershire but work at Sutton Walls, some 15 miles west of the county boundary, suggests that half the animals were cattle, a third sheep and a sixth swine.

Artefacts and utensils give glimpses of the Iron Age life-style. Finds of weaving combs and loom weights prove that the basic skill of cloth-making had been mastered. Regional types of pottery can now be distinguished by means of the rock fragments included as tempering. Two widespread varieties emanated from the Malverns, both made by professional potters. One of these was tempered by Malvernian rock fragments and has linear tooled patterns, while the other used Silurian limestone and was stamped with repetitive decorative motifs. Currency bars have been found in several places, showing that trading had progressed beyond the early systems of barter. By this time there was a system of trackways across the county, some of them converging on Droitwich, where there is evidence of Iron Age salt working.

Commercial activities and the need to control the crossing point of the Severn might have caused the first growth of a permanent settlement at Worcester at this time. A ditch excavated at Lich Street, just north of the cathedral, contained pots that can be dated between 400 and 100 B.C., whereas all evidence of earlier activity occurs further away from the city centre.

The most spectacular remnants of the Iron Age are the great hill forts, of which remnants of at least 15 survive in Worcestershire. Most of these are situated on high land in strategic positions, such as Herefordshire Beacon and Midsummer Hill on the Malverns or Wychbury Hill near Hagley, part of the range dividing the Severn and Trent basins. Others are lower but control important routeways, for instance Gadbury Camp near Eldersfield, which controls the route from the south-west between the Severn and the Malverns. Some of the forts occupy hilltop sites, but others are on promontories, as at Kempsey just south of Worcester, or have higher land behind as at Conderton Camp on the southern slopes of Bredon Hill. In some cases substantial earthworks remain, as at the two forts on the Malverns or at Kemerton Camp at the summit of Bredon Hill. Elsewhere, only part of the ramparts survives as at Areley Wood near Bewdley, or has been ploughed out altogether, as at Solcum Farm, Wolverley, where a promontory fort once had three banks and ditches. The forts varied greatly in size, one of the largest being Woodbury Hill, Great Witley, which covers an area of 26 acres, whereas Garmsley Camp in the parish of Kyre Magna is only nine acres.

Some of these great earthworks may have been the strongholds of tribal chieftains. In all cases where excavation has taken place, evidence of permanent settlement has been found. At Midsummer Hill, where nearly all the ground is sloping, 230 hut terraces have been identified on that part of the hill free of dense vegetation, while excavation in a sample area has revealed a high density of buildings, with little clear space between them. The camps were probably used for trade and it has been argued that as the guard rooms at the camp entrances were not strong enough for military purposes, they may have been used to levy tolls. In some respects, however, the defences were very strong, often with two lines of ditches and ramparts, as on the vulnerable south side at Wychbury Camp. This fort has two exceptionally well preserved 'inturned entrances' where the timber gateways had to be attacked up a long, narrow passage, with ramparts protecting the defenders on either side.

Traditionally, most of these forts were ascribed to the first or second centuries B.C. but recent work has shown that some of them are much older, in some cases perhaps dating back to the late Bronze Age. The origin of some forts is complex. Conderton, for example, began as a cattle enclosure, part of which was later adapted for human habitation. At Kemerton Camp the outer line of earthworks is now thought to be the earlier, probably dating from the fourth or third century B.C. The inner defences, where the inner side of the ditch and the outer side of the rampart form an almost precipitous slope, were added later, to make the upper part of the fort more secure.

The distribution of coins and the availability of written sources from the early Roman period gives some knowledge of the tribal structure in the late Iron Age. Much of Worcestershire probably came under the rule of the Dubonni, who had their capitals in Gloucestershire. They were prolific builders of forts and probably built most of those in Worcestershire. Wychbury, which faces north, may have been part of their northern frontier. North-west Worcestershire, however, probably came under the influence of the Cornovii, who were based in Shropshire and Cheshire. Late in the Iron Age, much of the territory of the Dubonni was overcome by the advanced people known as the Belgae, who already ruled a large part of south-eastern England. The great hill fort at Kemerton was certainly taken in battle at this time, for the main inner gateway was burnt to the ground, while about 50 skeletons hacked by sword cuts were found in a ditch.

The Romano-British period

The Roman invasion of Britain in A.D. 43 quickly led to the defeat of the British forces in the south-east. By A.D. 47 a frontier had been established along the Jurassic escarpment, the subsequent line of the Fosse Way. This road just misses the main area of Worcestershire though it crosses some of the former outlying parishes of Blockley and Tredington. Here the Romans halted for three years, to build the Fosse Way as a supply road and to consolidate their hold over south-eastern England.

In A.D. 50 the advance was renewed but the main thrust was north of Worcestershire, along the route later followed by Watling Street and now by the A5. There was probably bitter fighting against the Cornovii, but eventually an outpost was established at Viroconium, which became one of the major towns of Roman Britain, and a base for operations against the Welsh. There was no centre of comparable importance in Worcestershire but first-century forts were certainly established at Droitwich and Grimley, and perhaps at Worcester and Clifton-on-Teme.

Troops based at these and other West Midland forts helped to subdue the Welsh before A.D. 100. The uneasy peace was broken about A.D. 155, when the Welsh may have burnt part of the civilian settlement at Worcester and caused a second refortification of the fort at Droitwich. The third and fourth centuries were more peaceful, but the area was always transitional between the well Romanised regions to the south-east and the uplands to the west which were largely under military rule. Romano-British is therefore a better term for this period than just Roman.

16 *A restored Roman mosaic found at Droitwich in 1847*

There is little evidence that the rural landscape was much affected by Roman rule. In the Vale of Evesham, where aerial photography has revealed many sites, it is the continuity of settlement which is most apparent. Houses were crude wooden structures, with wattle and daub walls and thatched roofs, similar to those of the pre-Roman period. Yet on some sites, as at Wickhamford, finds of roofing and flue tiles and of wall plaster show that superior buildings were erected, especially in the third and fourth centuries. Near Droitwich, three large villa-type houses have been identified, which had the character of winged corridor villas, complete with hypocausts, mosaic floors and painted wall plaster. The residents had a life-style comparable with that of the Romano-British élite in the south-east and may have been officials associated with brine extraction. The presence of the Romans certainly created a buoyant market for corn and livestock and stimulated trade in other ways, so that luxury items like glass beads are sometimes found. The process was perhaps one of very gradual 'Romanisation', though the remarkable discovery of some 400 gold coins and 2,000 silver coins at Cleeve Prior in 1811 shows that there were opportunities to accumulate great wealth.

The Romans certainly expanded the manufacture of pottery in the Malverns, using the same clay as their Iron Age forebears. The sites of six pottery kilns and of one tile kiln have been discovered. Products have been found at 23 military and civil sites throughout Worcestershire and Herefordshire, thinning out eastwards into Warwickshire, northwards into Shropshire and Staffordshire and westwards into south-east Wales. A detailed study of the kiln site at Great Buckman's Farm

17 Markings of a Roman fort, at Upper Sapey, Clifton-on-Teme. This was probably in use after A.D. 150. and may have been manned intermittently by small units with a police function

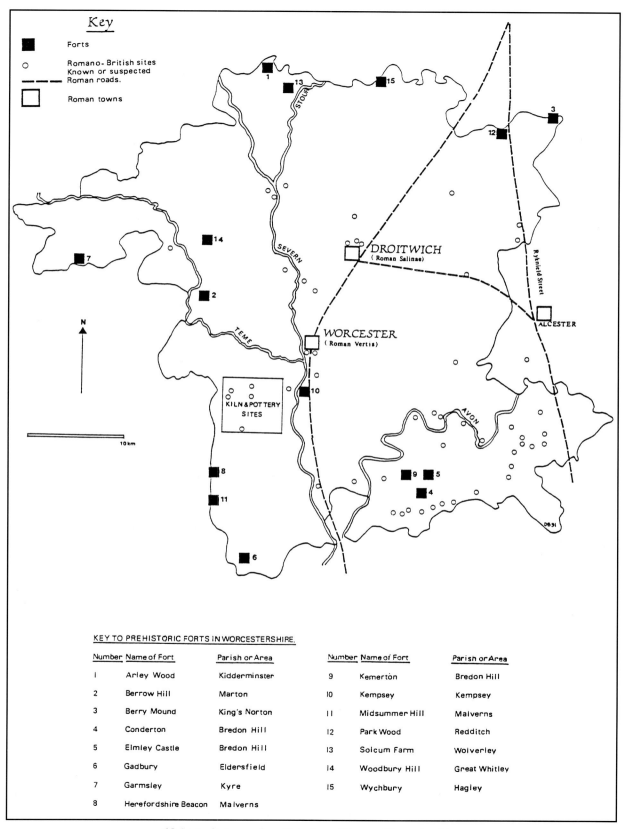

Key

■ Forts

○ Romano-British sites
  Known or suspected

- - - Roman roads.

☐ Roman towns

1

13

15

STOUR

3

12

14

7

SEVERN

DROITWICH
(Roman Salinae)

2

N

TEME

WORCESTER
(Roman Vertis)

Ryknield Street

ALCESTER

10

KILN & POTTERY
SITES

10 km

AVON

8

9   5

4

11

6

DB 91

KEY TO PREHISTORIC FORTS IN WORCESTERSHIRE.

Number	Name of Fort	Parish or Area	Number	Name of Fort	Parish or Area
1	Arley Wood	Kidderminster	9	Kemerton	Bredon Hill
2	Berrow Hill	Marton	10	Kempsey	Kempsey
3	Berry Mound	King's Norton	11	Midsummer Hill	Malverns
4	Conderton	Bredon Hill	12	Park Wood	Redditch
5	Elmley Castle	Bredon Hill	13	Solcum Farm	Wolverley
6	Gadbury	Eldersfield	14	Woodbury Hill	Great Whitley
7	Garmsley	Kyre	15	Wychbury	Hagley
8	Herefordshire Beacon	Malverns			

18 *Some features of prehistoric and Roman Worcestershire*

19 A stretch of straight road following a Roman alignment just west of Feckenham. This was later one of the salt roads which radiated from Droitwich

has shown that seven main types of vessels were produced, including tankards, flagons and different types of bowls and jars.

The large quantity of Roman pottery and the long series of coins found on the southern part of medieval Worcester suggest that there was intensive and continuous occupation of the site. This has been identified as the Roman town of *Vitris*, though it was never as large or as important as Gloucester or Wroxeter. It would have been logical to build a fort here in or soon after A.D. 50, as one of a line of Roman control points along the Severn. Yet evidence of this remains elusive. The civilian settlement that came later may have begun within the semicircle bounded by the Iron Age ditch. The area enclosed is roughly defined by Copenhagen Street, Friar Street and Severn Street. It is not known if the town was ever walled but there was a north-eastern gateway near the junction of Pump Street and High Street, for here a thick cobbled surface eight feet below present street level is thought to mark the point where the road from Droitwich entered the town. No traces of public buildings or of luxury houses with mosaics have yet been found, and it may be that *Vitris* was entirely a timber town. There was a burial ground just outside the ditch to the south and an extramural suburb to the north, centred on Broad Street, where iron working was practised.

I *Broadway Tower on the edge of the Cotswolds escarpment, with the Vale of Evesham beyond. The tower was built in 1800 as a folly by the Earl of Coventry*

II *The Malvern Hills from the path to Herefordshire Beacon. These ancient rocks, metamorphosed by great heat and pressure, have been faulted and fractured into an inclined slice of hard rocks resistant to erosion. They form a prominent western boundary to the historic county and today are a greatly valued leisure amenity*

III *The Staffordshire and Worcestershire Canal, built by James Brindley between 1766 and 1770, entering the River Severn. The canal enabled bulky goods to be transported onto and away from the Birmingham plateau. The new town of Stourport-on-Severn quickly developed where the canal joined the Severn*

IV *The River Severn from Holt Fleet Bridge near Ombersley. Long used as a major artery of trade, the Severn was greatly improved for navigation following a Parliamentary Act in 1842*

Chapter 3

Saxons, Hwicce and Danes, 410-1066

The Saxons

The history of the years after the withdrawal of the last Roman garrisons in A.D. 410 is confused and uncertain, in Worcestershire and elsewhere. Raiders had been troublesome since the third century B.C., especially the Picts and the Scots. The first Germanic settlers may have been mercenaries, enlisted by the Romans to repel this threat from the north and west. After 410 the Anglo-Saxons came in greater numbers, at first peacefully, but later as conquerors, as the Romano-British system of law and order degenerated, and as plagues weakened resistance. In the sixth century a British monk, Gildas, wrote of the 'fire heaped up and nurtured by the hand of the impious easterners ... which devastated town and country round about'.

    The old order may have lasted longest in Gloucestershire and Worcestershire, the area once ruled by the Dubonni. Their territory lay some distance from Irish inroads in the west and from the Anglo-Saxons established in the south and east. When penetration did occur, it is likely to have come from the Saxons, who were settled in southern England, rather than from the Angles, who were further east. It was probably by gradual infiltration, rather than by sudden conquest. This is shown by the Celtic place-name Pensax, a hamlet in the north-west of the present

20 Pensax Hill, seen from a steep sided valley to the west. The study of place-names suggests that this was one of the first areas to be colonised by the invading Saxons, perhaps in the sixth century A.D.

county, which means 'hill of the Saxons'. Their presence there was unusual enough and long enough to give the settlement its name. High up between the valleys of the Severn and the Teme, the advantages of this site would have attracted immigrants, not quite sure of their reception in an alien countryside! Place-names like Walmer and Walcot, meaning 'the pool of the Welsh' and 'cottage of the Welsh', referring to places a few miles east of the Severn, reflect a later phase of the process, when it was the Celts or Welsh who were the minority group.

21 A view from the triangular market-place at Tenbury Wells, looking up Church Street towards St Mary's parish church. This may have been a small Anglo-Saxon market town, to which the Normans added Teme Street, with its regular burgages

The Hwicce

Whatever form the integration of British and Saxon may have taken, a decisive event occurred in 577, when the West Saxon king, Cealwin, won a great victory over the Britons at Dyrham in south Gloucestershire. Within a generation a new kingdom had emerged, that of the Hwicce, who eventually ruled what became Gloucestershire and Worcestershire and the western part of Warwickshire, that is the area later covered by the medieval diocese of Worcester. The origin and composition of the Hwicce have been keenly debated by scholars but they seem to have come from both Saxon and British stock, though it is likely that Saxon overlords were the driving force in establishing the new kingdom.

The Hwicce formed a buffer between the British in the west and the new kingdom of Mercia, which occupied much of central England including the greater part of Warwickshire. *The Anglo-Saxon Chronicle* reports that in 628, Cyngelis, the leader of the West Saxons, was forced to come to terms with Penda, the leader of the Mercians. It is probable that the Hwicce came under Mercian control at the same time, though they retained a separate identity until the close of the eighth century, when the royal genealogy suddenly ends. By that time Mercia was ruled by Offa the Great, who extended his domain to the border of modern Wales and built the great earthwork which still bears his name. But the memory of the Hwicce continued and as late as the 10th century the Bishops of Worcester were styled 'episcopi Hwicciorum'.

The Danes

The late eighth century also saw the first Danish raids on the east coast. These became more severe in the mid-ninth century and Mercia was invaded in 874. There is little evidence of Danish settlement in Worcestershire and Scandinavian place-names, such as those ending in '-by', are noticeably absent, but the indirect effects of the Danes were considerable.

As is well known, the English resistance was organised by Alfred, King of Wessex from 871 to 899. His daughter, Aethelflaed, married Ethelred of Mercia, who turned a number of pre-existing towns into a series of well defended burghs. The first of these was Worcester, where earlier defences were improved between

884 and 901. Ethelred died in 911 but his widow continued the work, refortifying Stafford, Tamworth and Warwick. By 918 the Danes had been completely driven out from Mercia, which was now part of an enlarged Wessex, ruled by Alfred's son, Edward the Elder. As though to emphasise the new start, the old Mercia was divided into the three new administrative areas of Staffordshire, Warwickshire and Worcestershire, each based on one of the new burghs and each taking a slice of the thinly populated upland later known as the Birmingham plateau.

The Landscape and the Economy

The role of the Anglo-Saxons in moulding the English landscape is still debated by scholars. Some stress the continuity of settlement and cultivation from prehistoric and Romano-British times, while others emphasise the extent of new colonisation. In Worcestershire, both processes occurred. Some archaeological evidence is available but for the most part researchers must rely on the interpretation of place-names. Many of these come from pre-Norman conquest land charters, which are prolific for Worcestershire.

Many British place-names survive, most of them referring to rivers and to other major topographical features. Malvern, for instance, derives from the Welsh 'moel', meaning bare, and the Welsh 'bryn', meaning hill. Such features were so well known that the new settlers retained the old names, rather as the English immigrants to North America adopted Indian place-names. Many other early Anglo-Saxon names were also topographical, as at Bredon, where 'dun', meaning hill, was added to the British 'bre', also meaning hill.

Two of the commonest terminations in place-names are '-tun', now usually 'ton', which means farm, village or estate; and '-leah', now 'ley', meaning wood, clearing or glade in a wood. The 'tun' names are most common in the south-east, in the areas which had a long tradition of settlement and cultivation. The prefix is often the name of a tribal leader, as at Eckington, 'the tun of Ecca's people', or Peopleton, 'the tun of Pyppel's people', after whom the ancient site was renamed. The 'leah' names, on the other hand, are densest in the west and in the north-east, where woodland persisted longest and where signs of earlier occupation are more scattered. Again, the term is often compounded with a personal name, but woodland activities are often featured. Thus Beoley, north-east of Redditch, was 'the beekeeper's clearing', while Areley, in the north-west of the county, meant 'the wood of the eagle'. Some scholars argue that '-leah' names are comparatively late, reflecting an expansion of settlement in the 10th and 11th centuries, but others prefer an earlier date.

The charters and other sources show that mixed farming was practised on many Worcestershire estates in the late Anglo-Saxon period. At Norton and Lenchwick, on the north bank of the Avon, part of an 11th-century estate carried six oxen, 20 sheep and 20 acres of sown corn. At Salwarpe, near Droitwich, meadowland for the support of livestock was next to 'the water-course of the barley clearing'. A common place element 'wick', though sometimes referring to salt production, often occurs in flat alluvial valleys, as at Wick just east of Pershore, and in that context is thought to refer to dairy farms. Charter references confirm that many estates in the fertile south-east were intensively cultivated. Ploughlands are recorded in abundance, sometimes stretching to the estate boundaries. Wheat,

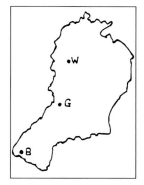

22   B: Bristol
      G: Gloucester
      W: Worcester
The medieval diocese of Worcester, which covered the area once settled by the Hwicce

23 The Danes crossed the North Sea in longships. Worcester was one of several burghs built to check their western expansion

barley, oats and rye are all mentioned in different charters, while at Tapenhall near Worcester there was a reference to 'the way to the flax acres'.

Aerial photographs often show strip cultivation in open fields in these areas but its precise dating is uncertain. There are charter references, however, which imply that farmers had land in different fields. Thus a 10th-century charter of Cudley near Worcester refers to '30 acres on the two open sharelands ...'. At Moreton in Bredon, on the other hand, there are suggestions of infield and outfield in the stipulation that two brothers, Beornheath and Brihtstan, should have three acres and one acre respectively, 'both central and outlying as pertains to the estate'. In some areas small enclosed fields were already a feature of the landscape, as at Huddington east of Worcester, where a charter refers to 'the barley croft' and 'the rye croft'.

The woodland areas had a different kind of economy. The wood itself was of great value, and rights of taking timber for building and fuel were often granted. Mast and acorns were valuable sources of fodder for the large herds of pigs pastured in the woods but this sometimes led to disputes. In 825 the swine-reeve of the King of Mercia tried to extend his swine pasture at Sinton in the parish of Leigh but was resisted by the Bishop of Worcester, who refused to give up more than 'mast for 300 swine'. Honey from wild bees was another woodland commodity and the numerous 'Honey' bournes and brooks may have been named after the wild bees which congregated on their banks. Sheep and cattle were also common and the true meaning of 'leah' is perhaps woodland pasture, rather than just woodland clearing.

Large tracts of woodland, however, were still undeveloped, as in the region of Wyre in the north-west. Deer, wild boar and even wolves are referred to in charters from these areas. The laws of Cnut show that hunting preserves had been set aside by the 10th century and hunting rights were sometimes included in a charter grant, as at Grimley just north of Worcester in the 10th century, when Bishop Oswald leased 'woods for hunting' to his brother Osulf. The only reference to a hunting park occurs in a ninth-century charter for Huddington in mid-Worcestershire, but 'hagas' or fenced enclosures were more common.

24 An artist's impression of an early Anglo-Saxon village. Later, most wooden churches were rebuilt in stone

Territories and Boundaries

The earliest pattern of territorial organisation seems to have been one of large estates, each of which contained different kinds of countryside, grouped together for the support of a ruler and his court through a system of tribute or service. These regions were sometimes contiguous, as in the territory called Husmere, which has left its name as Ismere, now a farm on the southern edge of Wolverley parish. Husmere included well developed lands near Kidderminster but also the wooded countryside of the Clent foothills. In other cases, territories were split geographically, as reflected in the grant in 875 of an estate at Overbury on the flanks of Bredon Hill, with which was associated the dependent vill of Pendock, on waste land near the Malverns.

By the time of the first charters in the eighth century these territories were becoming fragmented, as portions were granted to ecclesiastical bodies and other owners. An example is the estate of Wican, which was granted to the church of Worcester by Offa of Mercia between 757 and A.D. 775. This estate contained some of the 'weogorena leage', or 'the woodland of Worcester' in the west, as well as fertile lands along the River Severn, and was probably part of a larger territorial grouping which extended east of the river.

As the administrative system evolved, such estates were broken down into smaller units. The most fundamental of these was the township. Many of the parishes of Wican had more than one township, while in some charters the inhabitants of such communities are named. A charter of Lower Wolverton in Stoulton, south-east of Worcester, refers to 'the dyke of the Monninghaeme'. Some townships came to constitute individual manors, the holdings of lords, but others were merged for this purpose. Equally, some townships, especially in the more prosperous areas, became parishes in their own right, but others amalgamated to form larger parishes, as at Inkberrow near the eastern edge of the county.

At the other end of the scale, estates were amalgamated to form hundreds, each of which originally contained 100 hides (that is, enough land to support 100 households). Some of these formed massive blocks of land, like Came Hundred in the north-east, but others like Pershore and Oswaldslow were fragmented, reflecting holdings by great landlords, especially ecclesiastical bodies. The hundred courts were popular assemblies which met in the open at easily identifiable places. Two of the hundreds, Cresselau and Oswaldslow, have names which incorporate the element '-hlau' or tumulus, and the long barrow in Chaddesley Corbett may have been the meeting place for the former.

Because of the abundance of pre-1066 charters, Worcestershire is exceptionally well endowed with information about the boundaries between these territorial divisions. Without detailed maps, such boundaries needed to be easily recognisable. A fifth of them followed rivers and watercourses, especially in wooded areas, where some landmarks might be hidden. Others followed roads, especially the saltways radiating from Droitwich. Others, again, were created by man, such as the dykes dug round Martin Hussingtree, an island of Pershore Abbey land surrounded by the estates of the Bishop of Worcester. Point features, such as barrows, particular trees or ponds were also used, as were hung crucifixes on the boundary of church land at Grimley, Stoke Prior and Tardebigge. More surprising are the roe-deer's lair at Coften Hackett and the old manure heap on the boundary of Evesham lands.

25 *Christian missionaries evangelised Mercia in the seventh century, often preaching from pagan hill-top sites*

Christianity

The seventh century saw the spread of Christianity over most of Britain. Negotiations between the church promoted by missionaries from Rome and the old Celtic church culminated in the Synod of Whitby in 663, which drew up a common code of practice and administration. An earlier meeting had occurred in 603, when the missionary Augustine is said to have met leaders of the British church 'in confinio Huicciorum et Occidentalium Saxonum', 'on the border between the Hwiccas and the West Saxons'. In Mercia, Penda remained a pagan until his death in 654, but he did not restrict missionary activity and his heirs are said to have been Christian by the mid-seventh century. In 680, as part of the reorganisation of the church emanating from the Synod of Whitby, the previously large see of Mercia was subdivided, and the diocese of Worcester was created, with its bishop seated at

Worcester. The three bishops who held office during the first 12 years all came from the monastery of St Hilda at Whitby, which supports the tradition that the rulers of Mercia had been converted from Northumbria.

A number of place-names have a pagan origin, and though these may predate the adoption of Christianity, it is more likely that they show the persistence of paganism and pagan traditions, especially in the more remote parts of the county. 'Tyes mere', a pond in the ancient parish of King's Norton, is derived from the Anglo-Saxon 'Tiw', the god after whom Tuesday is also named. The element 'hlaw', referring to a pre-Christian tumulus or burial ground, occurs several times, as at Lowe Farm in Eardiston, overlooking the River Teme in the north-west.

To counteract such paganism, a number of minster churches were established, including that of St Peter at Worcester, which was used by the early bishops. From such churches, priests were sent out to evangelise the surrounding district and to found daughter churches. The areas covered by minster churches often corresponded to earlier tribal territories, as in the north-west of the county, where the modern rural deanery of Kidderminster marks the former territory of the Husmere.

No Saxon churches or parts of churches survive in Worcestershire but a few stone fragments give a hint of great artistic achievement. The finest is the ninth-century cross head at St Michael's, Cropthorne, where birds and beasts are intertwined with scrolls, and where a classical Greek cross is a surprising feature. At Frankley, in the far north, there is part of a cross shaft, though its interlacing ornament is badly weathered. There is similar interlacing at Rous Lench and on a reused stone at Stoke Prior. The Lechmere stone at Severn End House in Hanley Castle is part of a tomb and has a carving which is 'rather wild', probably 11th-century, showing an unidentified figure with a large headdress.

The first age of Christianity in England was one of great monastic fervour. The monasteries came late to Worcestershire, reflecting its late conversion, but the foundations eventually made at Worcester, Pershore and Evesham were long lasting and rich. Bede's *Ecclesiastical History,* completed in 731, reports that the bishop's church at Worcester, dedicated to St Peter, was served by both secular priests and monks, secular priests being those who had not taken the vows of chastity, obedience and poverty. From 743, however, there was a separate monastic community at a neighbouring church, St Mary's, and this later became the bishop's seat and the ancestor of the present cathedral. There was a similar pattern at Pershore, allegedly founded in 689 by a nephew of the King of Mercia. It was first staffed by secular canons but monks were introduced later. Evesham was the last to be founded, following a royal grant in 701, Bishop Egwin resigning his see to become the first abbot in 710.

The monasteries attracted many endowments in the early years. Evesham, for example, had 120 properties by 714, while most of the estates in the fragmented hundred of Pershore were owned by the abbey. Yet all experienced many vicissitudes. There were periods of internal slackness and many threats from outside. In the 10th century Oswald, bishop from 959 to 991, introduced stricter Benedictine rule at Worcester, while in 972 Pershore was refounded as a Benedictine house. A few years later, however, Evesham suffered interference from Adulf of Peterborough, who was bishop from 992 to 1002, while in the 1040s

26 Ninth-century cross head at St Michael's, Cropthorne, near Pershore

much of its land was seized by Earl Godwin, a magnate powerful enough to threaten even the king. William of Malmesbury, a 12th-century chronicler, reports even greater disasters at Pershore, which had losses amounting to 'more than half her revenues, one part being devoured by the ambition of the rich ... another bestowed by Edward the Confessor ... on Westminster'.

The Towns and Trade

Before the 10th century, Worcester alone could be called a town. Even here the evidence of continuity from the Romano-British period is slight. The choice of Worcester as the seat of the bishop in 680 suggests strongly, however, that this was the most important central place in the diocese. By the early eighth century Worcester had two churches as well as the cathedral, and a charter that can be dated earlier than 745 describes it as a metropolis or capital.

27 *A Saxon king and some of his courtiers*

The refortification of Worcester as a burgh between 884 and 901 was a major stage in its growth. The defences seem to have been inside the medieval town, though there were a number of realignments. The town had an established market function, for a charter divides fines for 'theft or dishonest trading' between the church of St Peter and the royal patrons. Alone of pre-Domesday Worcestershire towns, the new burgh had a mint, and in 904 there is the first of several references to property holdings. Later in the century it had a new cathedral, for soon after his enthronement in 960 Bishop Oswald transferred his seat to St Mary's, and began a rebuilding, not finished until 983. The cathedral then had 28 altars, but nothing now remains except a few turned capitals in the passage leading out of the present building past the chapter house.

The increase in trade in the 10th century probably stimulated the beginnings of other towns, and pre-Conquest features can be recognised in some town plans. In 909 there is a single reference to Bromsgrove as Bᵣ mesesburh, possibly an indication that it too was given defences against the Danes, perhaps as a temporary feature. The semicircular street and plot pattern between the High Street and the large churchyard may fossilise some early earthwork. Evesham and Pershore were the centres of great monastic estates and, in both early market-places can be detected outside the abbey precincts. At Evesham this was perhaps the open space preserved as Merstow Green; at Pershore it is the triangle north of the abbey. Early trading places, on the coast or inland, were known as ports, and the fact that a routeway recorded as 'the port way' in an 11th-century charter for Pensax seems to be leading to Tenbury has led to the suggestion that here too there may have been a market function before the later development by the Normans.

Droitwich continued to enjoy a unique role on account of its salt deposits and probably attracted other market functions. Eighth-century charters refer to salt works where the brine was boiled in leaden pans on ovens fired by wood or coal. These were sited in simple buildings referred to in the charters as *casulae*. A later charter shows that the salt was carried by pack-horse and cartload, and that tolls were payable called 'waggon-shilling' and 'pack-load penny'. Trade routes reached as far afield as Northamptonshire and Somerset, and coins have been found dating back to 740.

Chapter 4

The Norman Conquest and
Domesday Worcestershire, 1066-86

28 An 18th century view of Dudley Castle, showing its fine natural position on a ridge of Silurian limestone

The victory of Duke William of Normandy over King Harold at Hastings on 14 October 1066 brought a new aristocracy of some 5,000 barons and knights to England. The Normans soon conquered the greater part of the English lowlands. There was fierce fighting in some areas, including parts of Stafford-shire, Shropshire and Herefordshire, but in Worcestershire there was little resistance. The conquered land was quickly shared out among the great barons who had supported William, and they in turn distributed estates among the vassal knights who had supported them. The new overlords built castles, usually beginning with a quickly constructed 'motte and bailey', stone structures coming later.

The most powerful Norman in Worcestershire was Urse d'Abitot, who was appointed sheriff by William. He eventually held about a sixth of the county, either direct from the king or as a subtenant. In 1069 he built a motte and bailey castle in the south-west corner of Worcester, but found it necessary to cut off a slice of the cemetery of the Benedictine monks who used Worcester Cathedral as their priory church. This action brought him the contumely of the church, Archbishop Aldred of York condemning him with the words: Hightest thou Urse? Have thou Godes kurs!

Other castles built by the first generation of Normans included that of William fitz Ansculf on a superb natural site at Dudley, and that of Robert Despenser, William the Conqueror's Steward, at Elmley Castle, on the slopes of Bredon Hill. Some Norman work survives in the gatehouse at Dudley but at Elmley Castle only a few stones remain. Worcestershire, in fact, has very few castle remnants, though Norman mottes and some other earthworks survive at Clifton-on-Teme, Rochford and Tenbury, all in the north-west of the county.

Although there was some spoliation by the Normans, the Church retained most of its land after the Conquest, as is shown by Domesday Book in 1086. The Church owned nearly two-thirds of the county, having 786 of the 1,200 hides, the units of assessment into which the county was divided. Nearly all of this was held by the great religious houses of Worcester, Evesham and Pershore, and by Westminster Abbey, which had been given much of the Pershore Abbey estate by Edward the Confessor. Rivalry between the houses continued, however, and Domesday Book records that the ownership of a hide at Bransford, in the south-west of the county, had been disputed between Evesham and Pershore.

   Much of the credit for the way in which the Church asserted its claims in
Worcestershire must go to Wulstan, a monk of great piety who was Prior
at St Mary's, Worcester, and who became Bishop of Worcester in 1062. He was
one of only two Saxon bishops in the country to retain his office after the Conquest.
This was partly because of his early submission to the Normans, partly because of
his popularity and holiness. Wulstan supported the Normans on a number of
occasions, as in 1088, when he hurled a curse at the Welsh rebels led by Roger
Montgomery, and gave a blessing to the troops of William Rufus, the Conqueror's
successor. Contemporary chroniclers attributed the Norman victory to these
actions, and Wulstan's death in 1095 was lamented by Normans and Saxons alike.
   The rest of the county was held either by the king or by the lay lords who
had displaced the Saxon thegns. The royal manors formed a broken crescent
round all the county except the south-east. Most of them were forested areas,
with a great potential for hunting. The lay estates were all in the northern half
of Worcestershire, but most lords lived outside the county. One such absentee
was Ralph of Tosney, who had 15 holdings in Worcestershire, but whose main
seat was at Flamstead in Hertfordshire. Others, such as Ralph Mortimer of
Wigmore and Richard Fitz Osbern of Richards Castle, were marcher lords living
on the Welsh border.

Domesday Worcestershire

The difficulties of analysing and interpreting Domesday Book, commissioned by
William the Conqueror at Gloucester late in 1085, are enormous, but the document
does provide a unique glimpse of the county at the beginning of the medieval
period.

   For most rural communities, the number of villeins (or villagers), bordars (or
smallholders) and slaves (or serfs) were listed. Villeins were the most favoured
peasant group, holding up to 30 acres in the common fields. In return for this, they
owed service to the manor, usually paid by working on the lord's lands for an
agreed number of days. Bordars also had feudal duties, but their land-holding was
smaller, often about five acres. The lowest status group was the serfs, who rarely
owned land, and spent most of their time working on the demesne, that is land
farmed directly by the lord of the manor or his bailiff. Some villeins and bordars
must sometimes have practised other crafts but these were not always listed, as is
shown by the fact that there were 104 mills, but only three millers. There are
occasional references to a bee-keeper, a huntsman and a cowman, and to two
dairymaids and eight swineherds, as well as to 61 priests, an unusually large
number for a Domesday county. Again, the number of village officials listed—15
reeves and five beadles—was larger than for many counties.

   Of the 4,341 persons noted in Domesday Worcestershire, 1,717 were bordars,
1,604 were villeins, and 704 were serfs, the remaining 316 forming a miscellane-
ous group. Worcestershire is unusual in being the only Midlands county which had
more bordars than villeins, the average ratio being nearly one bordar to two
villeins. The only towns listed were Worcester, Droitwich and Pershore, but in
each case the record is ambiguous. Both Worcester and Droitwich had at least 150
houses, but Pershore was smaller, with only 28 burgesses recorded.

29 St Wulstan, Bishop of Worcester 1062-85, portrayed in late 15th-century glass at Great Malvern Priory

Apart from the priests and perhaps some of the serfs, all the persons listed seem to have been heads of household, but in the absence of clear evidence of household size, the total population can only be estimated. Most scholars agree that the average household size is unlikely to have been more than five. This means that the county's population was probably no more than 23,000, rather less then the population of Great Malvern at the present time. Whatever the total may have been, comparison of the Domesday data shows that Worcestershire's population was little more than half that of Gloucestershire, and about two-thirds that of Warwickshire, but was only a little below Shropshire and Herefordshire, and rather more than Staffordshire.

The density of population, predictably, was greatest in the south-east, in the fertile valleys of the Severn and Avon, where the density was probably over 10 people a square mile. Here the proportion of ploughteams in demesne, operated directly for the lord of the manor, was higher than elsewhere, indicating a highly developed feudal structure with a large number of both villeins and serfs. In the manor of Lenchwick and Norton, for example, there were 16 ploughs, five of which were held by the lord, the Abbot of Evesham, while 10 of the 37 persons listed were slaves. In such manors arable farming was well developed, though in some cases there are hints of large-scale livestock farming, as at Powick, where there were 20 acres of meadow.

In less favoured areas, mostly those held by lay owners, a much higher proportion of the ploughteams was held by the villeins, and serfs occurred only rarely. In the manor of Wychbold, for example, just south of Bromsgrove, the lord, Richard fitz Osbern of Richard's Castle, had only one plough, whilst the 19 villeins and the 27 bordars had 18 ploughs between them. On the northern and western edges of the county, especially on royal manors such as Hanley Castle and Martley, a woodland economy prevailed, with at least a quarter of the land wooded. Here bordars were the largest group, with serfs almost completely absent. The demesne interest was minimal, with money rents replacing services in some cases, and with few or no demesne ploughteams.

Chapter 5

The Middle Ages, 1086-1485

People and the Land, 1086-1100: A Period of Expansion

Between 1100 and 1300 the population of England probably increased from about two million to about five million. A comparable increase occurred in Worcestershire, where the recorded tenants on 18 manors of the Bishop of Worcester rose from 950 in 1086 to 1,853 in 1299.

There was little if any improvement in the efficiency of farming. Crop yields were about a quarter of what they are today, and soil fertility was only maintained by leaving land fallow every second or third year. Increased production could only be obtained only by extending the area of cultivation. That this occurred in Worcestershire is shown by the large number of assarts, new areas of cultivated land cleared from woodland or the waste. On the bishop's estates these occurred principally in the Severn valley in the 12th century, but by the 13th century the emphasis shifted to the underdeveloped north and west of the county. Some assarts were added to the demesne, that is the land farmed directly for the bishop, but the great majority, totalling many hundreds of acres, were created and worked by tenants, who often held free tenures for cash rents.

30 Castlemorton Common. This is the last extensive relic of Malvern Chase, a tract of land between the Malvern Hills and the River Severn. Here strict hunting laws persisted for many centuries and much of the land remained wooded or waste

31 *The deserted medieval village of Sheriff's Naunton, now part of the parish of Naunton Beauchamp, a few miles east of Worcester*

A study of the elongated parish of Yardley, in the north-east of the medieval county, illustrates the way in which less favoured areas were colonised. In 1086 the population was about fifty, with up to 10 homesteads forming a small village in the north of the parish. A late 13th-century subsidy roll and other evidence suggest that by 1300 the population had risen to about 750. Three hamlets, each with open fields, had been established by communal effort in the north of the parish. In the south, individual families, with great physical effort, had assarted a previously uncleared forest area, giving a scatter of isolated farms which survived until the 19th century. The preponderance of place-name elements such as 'hurst' (wood), 'ley' (clearing) and 'hay' (from the Old English 'haeg' meaning enclosed piece of land) tell evocatively of the way in which this land was won. In 1221 the pressure on space in the south of the parish was already severe, for when Thomas de Swaneshurst made an assart on the waste, his hedges were pulled down by 19 of his neighbours, fearful for the pasturing of their own animals. A similar process was occurring in other underdeveloped regions, as in the great hunting area of Malvern Chase. As early as 1154 the Crown received the considerable sum of £33 16s. for licensed assarts, representing clearings of about 2,500 acres, a quarter of the whole Chase.

The People and the Land, 1300-1485: Crisis and Contraction

Though areas such as Wyre Forest remained under-developed, the extent of farm land in Worcestershire was probably near its limit by 1300. Yet the agricultural surplus was small. Nearly half the manorial tenants were living off 15 acres or less, and, given the low crop yields and their compulsory feudal payments, they teetered on the edge of subsistence.

In a good year like 1288, when wheat sold at 2d. a bushel, all was well, but a series of bad harvests brought disaster. Due to appalling weather, the harvests failed in 1315, 1316, and again in 1322, when the price of corn reached 3s. a bushel. There were widespread animal diseases, which reduced the wool clip and caused a shortage of draught-animals. Disease smote a hungry population, culminating in the Great Plague, which was at its height in 1349. In Worcester, burials were forbidden in the cathedral cemetery for fear of infection, and corpses had to be taken beyond the walls. The Bishop's Registers show that between July and December new clergy were presented to 67 of the 138 parishes, the death rate among clerics being very high. There was some recovery, but the cumulative effects of further plagues—in 1361-62, 1369 and 1375—left the population more than a third less than it had been in 1300.

Confirmation of this contraction comes from the 37 deserted settlement sites which have been identified in Worcestershire, many of them probably abandoned in the late 14th century. A few, like the earthworks by Church Farm at Knighton-on-Teme, occur on the upland edge of the county but the great majority are in the south-east. The largest cluster lies north of the Avon, between Worcester and the eastern county boundary, an area which still has an 'empty look' on a 1:50,000 O.S. map. Another group is south of the Avon, especially on the slopes of Bredon Hill.

In some cases, as at Grafton Flyford and Dormston, both just north of the A422 from Worcester to Alcester, an isolated church, sometimes with an adjoining 'Church Farm', provides a clear hint of a shrunken settlement, even before field work and aerial photography identify house platforms. Wollashill is a classic deserted village site, a mosaic of hollow ways and massive house platforms, on the northern slope of Bredon Hill. Elsewhere, part of a once larger village survives, as at Kington, south of the A422. Here the line of the modern road through the village is continued as an abandoned hollow way, with house and croft sites each side. Documentary evidence is sometimes available, as at Bickmarsh, north-east of Evesham, where there is now only a farm, but which had a chapel last recorded in 1325.

The fall in population and the withdrawal from marginal lands may have made life more secure for some people in the 15th century, but disease could still ravage the land and harvests still failed. In 1437, after heavy rains, the Prior of Worcester ordered the shrine of St Oswald to be carried in procession through the city, 'as we byn enformed that hyt hath byn afore this time for cessying of such continual reyne'. The worst year of the century was 1479/80, when the number of probates proved in the Worcestershire part of Hereford diocese was twice the annual average.

Lords, Peasants and Farming

The most progressive farming was that on the estates of the great landlords, especially the monastic houses. Records of seven manors of the Bishop of Worcester in the late 14th century show that the leading crops were wheat and barley, with legumes and oats some way behind, and only a little rye. In September 1389 there were 58 horses, 202 oxen, 159 cattle, 740 pigs and 4,638 sheep on the demesne lands of 16 of the bishop's manors. The last figure shows the increasing attention to sheep farming in the later Middle Ages, with landlords finding easy markets for wool, a situation that caused rural depopulation, though sometimes resulting from it. The manure of the animals fertilised the fields, and much of the barley, oats and legumes was used as fodder, with wheat surpluses sold for cash.

32 Clearing woodland to make an assart in the 13th century

33 *The huge 14th-century barn at Leigh Court, in the Teme valley, which was once part of the estates of Pershore Abbey. The barn is 150 ft. long, 34 ft. wide and about the same height. It has two porches large enough to accommodate loaded waggons*

34 *The interior of the barn, showing eight of its eleven cruck trusses. Apart from badly needed repairs a few years ago, this breathtaking building has hardly been altered since the 14th century*

Some of the profit from demesne farming was used for farm buildings. This can be seen from the records of Evesham Abbey, whose lands were among the most productive in the county. There are references to 14 barns, including 'the very fine one' of stone built at Middle Littleton in 1376. This and the later partly timber-framed building at Bretforton are still standing. So are the remarkable cruck barn at Leigh Court, on a manor of Pershore Abbey near the county's western boundary, which is more than 150 ft. long; and the aisled barn of the Bishop of Worcester at Bredon, dating from the first part of the 14th century. The monastic landlords also built a number of dovecotes, a privilege then reserved for manorial lords, monastic houses and parsons because of the damage done to crops. Another kind of capital investment was in artificial fishponds, fish having enormous importance in the medieval diet.

Peasant farming was generally less productive, with more emphasis on rye as a staple crop, especially on poorer, higher land. During the Middle Ages, labour services were gradually replaced by rents, and during the 15th century holdings became larger. Most smallholders and cottagers produced fruit, vegetables and hemp or flax from 'hemplecks', as well as cultivating strips in the open fields, and grazing animals on common land and on stubble 'after sickle'.

Rural society in medieval Worcestershire

Partly because of the large amount of land held by the church, the number of great magnates living in medieval Worcestershire was comparatively small, though some living elsewhere held estates in the county. The grandest were the Beauchamps, who were based at Elmley Castle, but owned land in more than 50 Worcestershire manors. In the mid-13th century, William Beauchamp married the heiress of the Earl of Warwick, and his son assumed that title, bringing the Beauchamps into the front rank of the English baronage.

At the same period there were about 50 Worcestershire families headed by knights. Originally, a knight was a mounted warrior with the right to bear helmet, haubeck, shield and lance, but by the late 13th century he had become a local administrator and justice of the peace, and was often the local representative of a great magnate. In 1275, 23 knights were put forward as jurors of the grand assize, including Richard of Ombersley, Adam of Elmbridge and Henry of Ribbesford. The 1275 subsidy return shows, however, that more than a third of villages had no resident who was a knight or in any sense 'gentry'.

Socially far below the magnates and the knights, were the peasants, the vast majority of rural population. They lived by cultivating a holding of usually scattered land and consuming much of the product. Poorer families worked for their richer neighbours or on the manorial demesne. The better-off peasant family lived in houses like that at Noake's Court at Defford, near Pershore. This is a three-bay house of cruck construction, about 37 ft. long. The top bay had a floored upper room but the other two bays formed a hall or living space open to the roof, heated by an open hearth. The remains of a 13th-century longhouse have been excavated at Upton, a hamlet in the Bishop of Worcester's manor of Blockley. Here, peasants and animals lived at different ends of the building but under one roof, each providing warmth for the other. No examples of humbler cottages or hovels have been found in Worcestershire, but living conditions must have been cramped and dismal.

A peasant dying at Wolverley in 1346 left a cart, a plough, a harrow and various tools. He had a vat, perhaps used for brewing, a trough, perhaps used for dough, a brass pot, a chest and a gridiron, with other small items. In 1393, a man arrested at Broadway for felony had a horse, a sword, a brass pot, a spit, a pair of cards for carding wool, a hatchet, and other items that gave the substantial value of £2 3s. 1d. In spite of the lack of a bed and other items of furniture, these were both 'well-to-do' peasants, and poorer families would have owned much less.

The Church

The pervasive power of the medieval Church is nowhere more apparent than in Worcestershire, where the great religious houses held more than half the land, and where the number of parish churches grew from about sixty in 1086 to over 135 by 1349. Piers Plowman was reflecting popular feeling when he condemned friars

35 *A peasant reaping the harvest with a sickle, as shown in a 15th-century Book of Hours*

36 *The stone barn at Middle Littleton, built by John Ombersley, Abbot of Evesham, in 1376*

37 A peasant and his cart, one of a fine series of 15th-century misericords at St Mary's church, Ripple

for 'preaching to the people for what they could get', while John Wycliff's denials of transubstantiation found many sympathisers in Worcestershire. Yet few challenged the basic assumptions on which the authority of the Church ultimately depended and excommunication was feared by almost everyone.

The feudal structure of secular society was matched by the church hierarchy, headed by the Bishop of Worcester. In the later Middle Ages many bishops were absentees, who ran the diocese through deputies. Philip Morgan (1418-25), for example, was consecrated at Rouen in Normandy, and spent most of his time in London, where he was a privy councillor. Many of his predecessors, however, resided in the county, two of the most powerful being Walter de Cantilupe (1237-66), who began to build an episcopal castle at Hartlebury, and Godfrey Giffard (1268-1301), who completed it. Some of the bishops were great statesmen, especially Cantilupe, who supported Simon de Montfort, and Adam Orleton (1327-33), who helped to dethrone King Edward II. Others are remembered as great builders. Few could equal the piety of Wulstan (1062-95), who was canonised in 1203 following a series of attested miracles at his tomb.

A number of royal occasions reflected the status of the cathedral, the headquarters of a large diocese as well as the church of St Mary's priory. Henry II and his queen Eleanor were crowned there for the third time in 1159. King John willed that he should be buried at Worcester and in 1216 his body was brought from Newark and buried in the chancel between the tombs of Oswald (959-91) and Wulstan, thus fulfilling an ancient prophecy that he would be buried among saints! The effigy, of Purbeck marble, is one of the finest of its time. In 1218 the church started by Wulstan was at last dedicated, in the presence of the young Henry III, nine bishops, 17 abbots and nine earls or barons.

The division of the huge diocese into two archdeaconries and their subdivision into deaneries probably began soon after 1066, but it is first recorded in a tax return of 1291. Except for the protruding parish of Broadway, which was in the Gloucester Archdeaconry, and the Deanery of Burford in the Hereford diocese, the whole of what later became the county of Worcester was in the Worcester Archdeaconry. This was divided into the deaneries of Droitwich, Evesham, Kidderminster, Powick and Worcester.

38 The end elevation of Noakes Court, Defford, showing a fine pair of crucks

The vitality of the Church in 12th-century Worcestershire can be seen in the quantity of Norman architecture. Norman work survives in about half the pre-Georgian churches in the county. Some Norman churches were remarkably large, as shown by the surviving naves at Bredon and Ripple, and by the largely Norman church still standing at Rock, with its richly decorated chancel arch. There are also several examples of high quality sculpture, sometimes showing Italian influences, as in the fine tympanum at Beckford; and a number of fine Norman fonts, as at Chaddesley Corbett, where four dragons are intertwined. After this burst of energy, there was less activity in the 13th and early 14th centuries, though high quality work sometimes reflects local affluence, as in the Decorated style east window at Chaddesley Corbett. From the 15th century there is fine perpendicular work, for example the slim tower at Romsley. Timber-framed towers and bell-turrets are a feature of the county, as at Dormston (dated *c*.1450) and Mamble. A new church at Kidderminster, now largely rebuilt, reflects the town life of 15th-century Worcestershire.

V *Worcester Cathedral was once the abbey church of a rich Benedictine monastery, as well as the seat of a bishop of a large medieval diocese. It has important parts in every architectural style from Norman to perpendicular. The handsome tower was completed in 1374, in spite of the economic difficulty following the Black Death*

VI *Load Street, Bewdley, in the 1820s. The shambles and other encroachments in this wide street market-place had been removed to other locations some years previously*

VII *The village of Elmley Castle, with the wooded slopes of Bredon Hill beyond. Vernacular buildings of varied local materials adjoin the wide central street, once used as a market-place*

The reforms of the more zealous bishops illustrate the problems of the medieval church, especially of inadequate or absentee clergy. In 1326 Bishop Cobham complained that the rector of the church of Hanbury 'makes no residence at his church but wanders about in London and elsewhere leading a most dissolute life'. The most far reaching measures were those taken by Bishop Cantilupe in the wake of the reforming Fourth Lateran Council of 1215. He drew up regulations to be observed by clergy in services and ritual, including such details as the new cloths to be worn by children at confirmation. Clergy were to guard against envy, and be regular in visiting the sick. Beginning in the mid-13th century, chantries were founded for the souls of deceased persons, often the local squire and his family. In 1448, for example, Eleanor, the wife of John Throckmorton, and her son Thomas endowed lands yielding £10 a year to support one chaplain to celebrate divine service at the altar of St Mary in memory of themselves, their ancestors and heirs.

39 A richly decorated late Norman doorway at St Peter's church, Rock, probably built c.1170

40 *A blocked doorway at St Mary's church, Ripple, in the Early English style of c.1230. The stiff-leaf foliage on the capitals is a prominent feature*

The religious houses

Monasticism in Worcestershire was dominated by the great Benedictine houses. The pre-Conquest foundations at Worcester, Evesham and Pershore were joined in 1085 by Great Malvern Priory and about 1115 by Little Malvern Priory, while later a Benedictine nunnery was established at Westwood, just north of Droitwich. Great Malvern, deliberately sited 'in that vast wilderness called Malvern', is reputed to have been started by Aldwin, a hermit monk under the influence of Wulstan of Worcester. Yet it became a subsidiary house to the great Abbey of Westminster, though Little Malvern was a cell of Worcester Priory.

Other orders established themselves in Worcestershire. These included a Cistercian Abbey at Bordesley in the parish of Redditch, founded in 1138, probably by the Empress Maud, and the Cluniac Priory of St James at Dudley, founded by Gervase Pagnal, the lord of Dudley Castle. A later foundation was at Halesowen in 1215, when the Bishop of Winchester founded a house of Premonstratensian Canons, following a gift of land from King John. There were also two small Cistercian nunneries, while at Astley, near Bewdley, there was a small priory of the order of St Benedict, dependent on an abbey in France.

None of the new foundations matched the endowed wealth of Worcester, Evesham and Pershore, though in 1291 Great Malvern had estates yielding £87 13s. 2d. a year. Bordesley, with £43 2s., and Dudley, with £27 11s. 4d., were well behind this figure, and some of the others were in continual financial difficulties, especially the Cistercian nunneries, one prioress complaining in 1308 that she was compelled to beg 'to the scandal of womanhood and the discredit of religion'.

Numbers are rarely recorded, but the biggest establishments seem to have been at Worcester and Evesham, the latter having 67 monks and 65 servants in the early 12th century. Bordesley, Pershore and Great Malvern had between 20 and 40 monks in the 13th century, but the only figures known for Halesowen and Little Malvern are below that figure. Records at Great Malvern give some information about 156 monks. Eighty-three of these were at the Priory for less than 10 years, most of them probably elderly men seeking a place of retirement late in life. The offices were usually held by younger men, some of whom stayed for very long periods, four being at Great Malvern for more than 50 years.

41 The east window at St Cassian's church, Chaddesley Corbett, where the chancel was rebuilt in the 14th century, using the Decorated style. The tracery is very complex and includes a roundel at the top, with four internal triangles

42 The south porch of St Egwin's church, Church Honeybourne, built in the Perpendicular style

The needs of these comparatively small communities were met by precincts of enormous size. Nothing survives in Worcestershire on the scale of the ruins at Glastonbury or Fountains, but the 14th- and 15th-century cloisters remain at Worcester, as do the Norman chapter-house and the later refectory. The entrance to the precinct was from the south-east, where the 14th-century Great Gate still stands. At Evesham, there are fragments of the late 13th-century chapter-house, and the Norman gateway which led from the town into the abbey is intact.

The main architectural styles are represented in the monastic churches of Worcester, Pershore and Great Malvern. At Worcester, the early Norman crypt dates from Wulstan's time. The chancel at Worcester, begun by William de Blois in 1224, is one of the masterpieces of the Early English style. At Pershore only the Early English chancel survives of the great medieval church, once 330 ft. long, and this was revaulted in the Decorated style after a fire in 1288, giving one of the earliest lierne vaults in England. The best Perpendicular work is at Great Malvern, where the nave was rebuilt in the 15th century. The stained glass and patterned tiles here are among the finest in England, showing that the greater glory of God was still an ideal in late medieval Worcestershire.

43 A stone effigy of a knight in the chancel of St Cassian's church, Chaddesley Corbett. It may be that of Roger Corbett, lord of the manor, who died in 1290. It was originally in the north chapel, which was built by the Corbett family in the 13th century as a manorial chapel

44 An alabaster effigy of a knight in St Peter's church, Martley. This is probably Sir Hugh Mortimer, Lord of Martley and Kyre, who was killed in the Battle of Wakefield, 1459, fighting for the Yorkist cause

45 The effigy of King John (d.1216), probably made about 1230. It lies on a 16th-century tomb chest in Worcester Cathedral

46 The richly decorated Norman font at St Cassian's church, Chaddesley Corbett. It dates from about 1165. There is interlacing on the base, plaiting on the stem and intertwined dragons on the bowl

The monastic system produced many devout men, including great scholars like Walcher of Lorraine (d.1135) of Great Malvern, who helped to spread the use of Arabic figures and degrees, minutes and seconds. There were also rows and scandals, as at Pershore in 1340, when there were complaints that certain brethren, 'degenerate sons', were wasting the abbey's goods by applying them to their own 'licentious pleasures'. The monasteries provided hospitality for travellers, and sometimes for pensioners and annuitants, as at Great Malvern in 1310, when the prior was ordered to provide a room and food for a retired royal servant.

The Friars

Worcester was an early centre for the Franciscans, who established themselves on the eastern side of the city near the city wall, giving their name to Friar Street. They followed the ideal of absolute poverty for Christ's sake and worked among the poor, especially lepers. Worcester became one of their centres in England. The friars won the support of the Beauchamps and other great families but were sometimes in conflict with the Benedictines over burial rights and other matters.

Over a century later the Dominicans or Black Friars arrived in Worcester, and secured land north of the city wall off what is now Broad Street. They too attracted support from the Beauchamps, but were generally less successful than the Franciscans. The only other friars in the county were the Austin Friars, who had a small house at Droitwich. All the friars were enthusiastic preachers, and spent much of their time out among the inhabitants of the towns.

The Hospitals

A remarkably early hospital was established in Worcester by Wulstan in 1085, on a site south-east of the city. This was later known as the Commandery, because from the late 13th century the Master was called Commander. In 1294, 22 sick persons could be accommodated. The present building is timber-framed and dates from the late 15th century, with a well preserved screens passage, though remains of an earlier chapel are set in the garden. There was another hospital in Worcester, dedicated to St Oswald, and first mentioned in 1268; and one at Droitwich, founded by the rector of Dodderhill.

Worcester City

Worcester was ranked tenth, equal to Gloucester, among the towns of 12th-century England, but by 1377 it had dropped to 25th, having developed more slowly than many towns, especially those in the more prosperous south-east. The population at that time was less than 2,500, the size of Upton-on-Severn today. By 1523, however, it ranked 16th, with a population climbing to about four thousand.

The plan of the city is puzzling, with the cathedral close occupying two-thirds of a semicircular Roman enclosure. High Street, running directly north from the close, may follow the line of a Roman road, while St Helen's church, dedicated to a Roman saint, adjoins this road inside the Roman defences. By 1086 the city had three churches, including St Helen's, and also St Martin's, perhaps the furthest point of expansion northwards at this time. A bridge was in existence by at least 1088, and there was a small suburb west of the Severn.

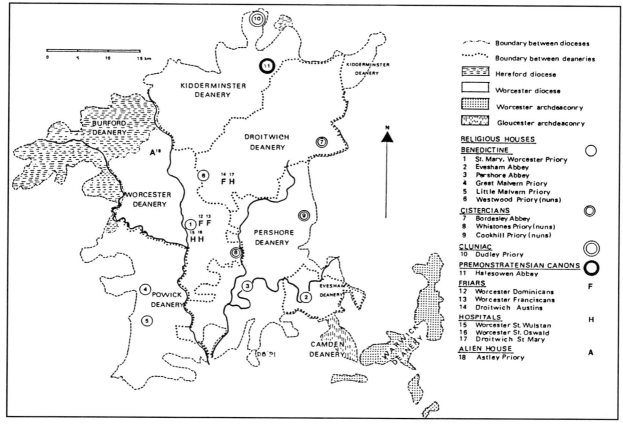

Legend:

- — · — · — Boundary between dioceses
- · · · · · · · · Boundary between deaneries
- Hereford diocese
- Worcester diocese
- Worcester archdeaconry
- Gloucester archdeaconry

RELIGIOUS HOUSES

BENEDICTINE ○
1. St. Mary, Worcester Priory
2. Evesham Abbey
3. Pershore Abbey
4. Great Malvern Priory
5. Little Malvern Priory
6. Westwood Priory (nuns)

CISTERCIANS ◎
7. Bordesley Abbey
8. Whistones Priory (nuns)
9. Cookhill Priory (nuns)

CLUNIAC ◉
10. Dudley Priory

PREMONSTRATENSIAN CANONS ○
11. Halesowen Abbey

FRIARS F
12. Worcester Dominicans
13. Worcester Franciscans
14. Droitwich Austins

HOSPITALS H
15. Worcester St. Wulstan
16. Worcester St. Oswald
17. Droitwich St Mary

ALIEN HOUSE A
18. Astley Priory

47 *Late medieval ecclesiastical divisions within Worcestershire*

In the 12th century Worcester was often burnt, and was captured by Matilda in 1139 and by Stephen in 1150, the latter easily entering the city because there were no defences on the north side. These were probably completed within a few years, for the main four gates are all referred to between 1175 and 1200. The walls were later rebuilt, following the first of a run of murage grants in 1224. The pattern of streets, some of which are named after medieval trades, is haphazard, though the line of Broad Street links East Gate with the bridge, intersecting High Street at the Cross. The earliest market-place, on the edge of the Saxon burgh north of what is now Broad Street, was built over in the 13th century, but a fragment survives as Corn Market.

Worcester gained a royal charter in 1189, giving it some independence of the Sheriff, and was created a Merchant Guild in 1227. Yet its constitutional development was slow. It was not formally incorporated until 1555 and did not become a mayoralty with county status until 1621, privileges gained much earlier by many cities.

Worcester has a number of fine medieval buildings, but mostly they relate to church institutions and hospitals. More knowledge of the city's economy can be gleaned from recent archaeology, as at a site in Sudbury, the suburb south-east of the cathedral. This revealed three craftsmen's tenements, aligned front end to the street, each with a minimum width of about 21 ft. There is evidence of bone-working from the 13th century, while in the 15th century two of the houses were occupied by bronze-smiths, who made articles ranging from large bells and cauldrons to small buckles and pendants.

48 *A monk working in the cloisters. The monks of Worcester produced a number of chronicles, including* The Annals of Worcester *in the early 14th century*

Other medieval towns

In Worcestershire, as elsewhere, many towns were founded or expanded during the 12th, 13th and 14th centuries. The development of towns was necessary to absorb surplus population from the rural manors, where pressure on the land was often intense. Tenants allowed to do so were eager to escape the feudal restrictions of the countryside, and the expression 'town air breathes free' was a popular maxim in the Middle Ages. Town growth or plantation was a profitable investment for manorial lords, who stood to benefit from the annual burgage rents paid by burgesses for their burgage plots, and from market tolls and court fines. Yet by modern standards none of the Worcestershire towns was large, the biggest after Worcester in the mid-16th century being Evesham with a population of about 1,400.

The distinction once made between towns which 'just grew' and planned towns is now regarded as an over-simplification. Many towns have an early urban core, to which planned units were added later. This probably occurred at Tenbury, where the Saxon settlement consisted of a short street from the church widening into a triangular market-place. After the Conquest the manor passed to the Clifford family, who eventually laid out a regular burgage series on either side of the present Teme Street, perhaps in 1248, when a Tuesday market and two annual fairs were granted.

Some of the most notable developments came from the church. At Evesham the abbey expanded the small pre-Conquest settlement northwards, with an irregular grid of streets, probably the 'new borough' which is referred to in a late 12th-century cartulary. A planned burgage series was also laid out east of the Avon, forming the separate vill of Bengeworth. At Pershore, the two abbeys of Pershore and Westminster developed separate burgage series along a curving street which bypassed the Saxon settlement, but shared the rectangular market-place. At Broadway, the Pershore monks paid 10 marks in 1196 for the privilege of holding a Wednesday market, at what was perceived as a good trading place, where the Cotswolds met the Vale of Evesham. The Bishop of Worcester developed a small town at Alvechurch, which was granted a market in 1239, and the see might also have been involved in Upton-on-Severn. One of the most obvious of planned towns is Halesowen, where the Abbot of Hales obtained permission to hold a market and fair in 1220.

Secular lords were no less active. Gervase Pagnal probably laid out a small town along a single street at the foot of Dudley Castle hill, while his successors, the Somerys, gave Dudley a charter in the 13th century, and also tried a less successful development at Clent. At Kidderminster, where the important pre-Conquest church was the urban nucleus, two lords founded a successful seigneurial borough. Two Herefordshire families were also active in Worcestershire. As well as extending Tenbury, the Cliffords tried unsuccessfully to found a town at Severn Stoke, while the Mortimers of Wigmore planted a new town at Clifton-on-Teme, which gained its market in 1270, and launched a more permanently successful venture at Bewdley. Here the new town was carved out of the old parish of Ribbesford in at least two stages, beginning up on the plateau near the hunting lodge of Tickenhill in the late 13th century, and expanding with a rectilinear plan in the Severn valley at a later date.

49 *The friars sang dirges round the bodies of rich men who willed to be buried in the friary churches. Such a burial was that of William Beauchamp, Earl of Warwick, at Greyfriars, Worcester, in 1298*

50 *The gateway to the Benedictine priory at Great Malvern, probably built in the late 15th century, in the Perpendicular style of the day. This drawing is by Henry Lamb, of the Royal Library, Malvern, who drew a number of local views and buildings in the mid-19th century. It shows the building as it was before battlements and other features were added in 1891*

51 *The chancel of the Benedictine abbey church at Pershore, consecrated in 1239, though the vault was rebuilt after a fire in 1288. The chancel is in the contemporary Early English style, with sharply pointed lancet windows, clusters of detached shafts around the columns, deep cut moulding on the arches and stiff-leaf carving on the capitals*

52 *This is a 19th-century drawing of a suggested reconstruction of the Guesten Hall (guest hall) of the great Benedictine abbey at Worcester. The hall was built in 1320, with a fine roof of open trusses and cusped braces and windbraces. The roof was taken down in 1861, repaired and reused in a new Worcester church. It is now proudly displayed in a new purpose-built hall at Avoncroft Museum of Buildings, near Bromsgrove*

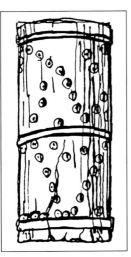

53 *Part of a 13th-century knife handle, 12 in., wide. It was found in 1972 in the middle of the three tenements at Sudbury*

Markets and Fairs

A weekly market and at least one annual fair were prerequisites of a successful town. Between 1150 and 1380, no less than 23 places in Worcestershire received charters for either a market or a fair, usually for both. In some cases, there was more than one charter, perhaps moving the market to a different day to avoid competition from a neighbour. Bromsgrove, for example, was granted a Wednesday market in 1300 but this was moved to Tuesday in 1317, perhaps because of the Wednesday market developing at Halesowen. Twelve of the 23 places received their first known market charter between 1210 and 1260, but three were granted after the Black Death, including the grant of a Wednesday market and two annual fairs at Bewdley in 1376.

Several of the places granted markets and fairs did not develop into towns. An example is Feckenham, a royal manor, which was granted a Thursday market and a fair in 1237. The Abbot of Evesham obtained a grant for a market and fair at Ombersley in 1354, but both had lapsed by 1535, probably having failed to compete with the well established market at Droitwich, only three miles down the road. A more spectacular failure occurred at Oldberrow, then a narrow tongue of Worcestershire protruding into the Warwickshire Forest of Arden. The Despensers obtained the manor from Evesham Abbey and were granted a market and fair here in 1253. The manor returned to Evesham Abbey in 1311, but there is no evidence that the market and fair were ever held, no doubt because there were six other markets in an area of less than 10 square miles.

The market space is a prominent feature of many towns. The simplest form is the widened street, which occurs at Bromsgrove, Droitwich, Dudley and Upton-on-Severn, and also at Broadway and Bewdley, though in those two cases the street widens into a triangle at one end. Rectangular market-places occur at Alvechurch, Kidderminster and Pershore, that at Kidderminster having entry streets at each corner. Triangular market-places can be found at Bengeworth, Clifton-on-Teme, Evesham and Tenbury.

Many market-places were colonised by stalls and booths, which eventually became permanent structures, in some cases paying rent to the borough or the manorial lord. This process was very marked in some of the monastic developments, as at Halesowen, where three blocks of small tenements almost fill the large triangular market-place. At Evesham, the famous Booth Hall is only one of a number of island blocks on what was originally a massive market-place, tapering northwards into the wide High Street. At Bewdley, St Anne's church, originally a chapel of ease without a churchyard, occupies the triangular part of the market-place, while a row of shambles and other structures extend down the middle of Load Street. The congestion must have been chaotic at times, an indication, perhaps, that Bewdley, benefiting from the river trade, became more successful than its planners anticipated.

Other urban functions and town government

All the successful towns had a range of trades, and during the medieval period a few of them began to develop reputations for specialist industries. As early as 1332, the townsmen of Kidderminster were making broad cloth and the narrower

54 *The High Street at Bromsgrove in the 1920s, showing the long, widened street used as the medieval market-place*

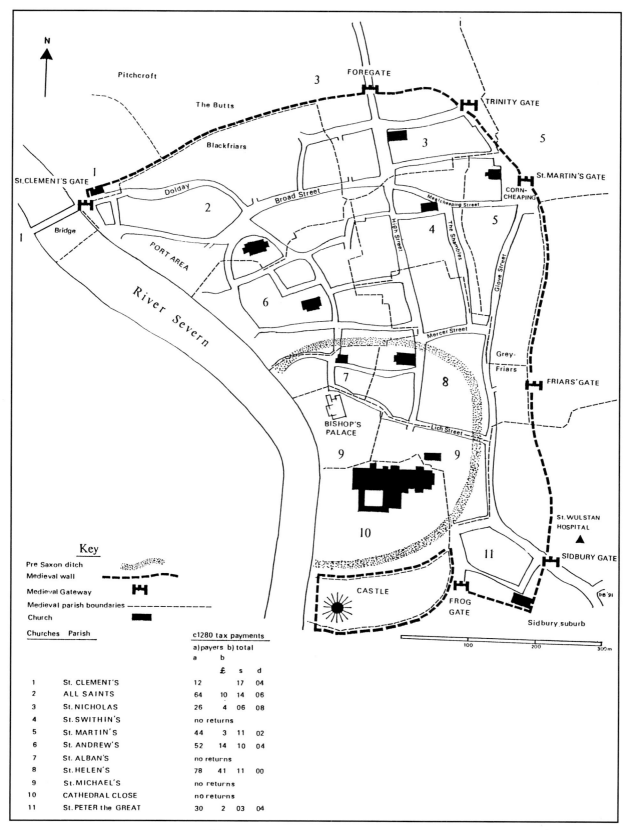

N

Pitchcroft

The Butts

Blackfriars

FOREGATE

3

TRINITY GATE

3

3

5

St. MARTIN'S GATE

St. CLEMENT'S GATE

1

Dolday

Broad Street

Mealcheaping Street

CORN-CHEAPING

1

Bridge

2

High Street

4

The Shambles

5

PORT AREA

Glove Street

6

Mercer Street

Grey-Friars

FRIARS' GATE

7

8

BISHOP'S PALACE

Lich Street

9

9

St. WULSTAN HOSPITAL

10

11

SIDBURY GATE

CASTLE

FROG GATE

Sidbury suburb

DB '91

River Severn

Key

Pre Saxon ditch	
Medieval wall	
Medieval Gateway	
Medieval parish boundaries	
Church	

100   200   300 m

Churches	Parish	c1280 tax payments			
		a) payers b) total			
		a	b		
			£	s	d
1	St. CLEMENT'S	12		17	04
2	ALL SAINTS	64	10	14	06
3	St. NICHOLAS	26	4	06	08
4	St. SWITHIN'S	no returns			
5	St. MARTIN'S	44	3	11	02
6	St. ANDREW'S	52	14	10	04
7	St. ALBAN'S	no returns			
8	St. HELEN'S	78	41	11	00
9	St. MICHAEL'S	no returns			
10	CATHEDRAL CLOSE	no returns			
11	St. PETER the GREAT	30	2	03	04

55 *Worcester City in the late Middle Ages*

56 *Map of central Pershore, showing the rectangular market-place (M) lying between the burgages of Pershore Abbey (unshaded) and those of Westminster Abbey (shaded)*

57 *The seal of the Borough of Droitwich. On the right two barrels of salt, still the town's chief product, are quartered with chequers, the symbol of the Droitwich Chequers where the salt accounts were made up*

kersey, while Dudley had its nailers in the 15th century. A genuine industrial town—one of only a very few in England at this time—was Droitwich, a major supplier of the salt which was vital to medieval society both as a condiment and as a preserver of meat and other foods. Each burgess had a right to about twenty quarters of brine per year. This was boiled and reduced to salt, which was then marketed, using roads which are still known by names such as Saltway. The prosperity of Droitwich can be seen by its payment of an annual fee farm of £100 to the exchequer, compared to £30 paid by Worcester.

Reflecting this prosperity, Droitwich received a borough charter in 1215, but progress towards self government was generally slow in Worcestershire towns. Smaller towns like Alvechurch always remained subject to a manorial court, as did some of the larger towns like Bromsgrove. Bewdley, which had passed from the Mortimers to the Crown, became a borough in 1472, but Evesham had to wait until 1605 and Kidderminster until 1636 to achieve that status, though their citizens had a large measure of independence long before that date.

Except for those of the church, few medieval buildings remain in Worcestershire towns, though some surprises lurk behind later façades, such as the fine base cruck at 7-10 Stourport Road, Bewdley, or the tunnel vault and 13th-century piscina at 21-25 High Street, Pershore. Town walls and other defences are rare in the county, though a stretch remains at Evesham, while some of the bridges are medieval, including those at Pershore and Tenbury.

The Battle of Evesham

One of the great battles of the Middle Ages took place in Worcestershire in 1265. It was the culmination of years of dynastic struggle under the weak rule of Henry III, king from 1216 to 1272. The rebel forces were led by Simon de Montfort, Earl of Leicester, the king's own brother-in-law, and included the Bishop of Worcester and other Worcestershire landowners. Earlier in the reign, de Montfort had served the King well by reasserting English rule in Gascony but he over-reached himself and tried to seize the crown. After defeating the court faction at Lewes in Sussex in 1263, he was temporarily in supreme power, which he used to summon together representative knights from the shires, an event regarded by some as the first Parliament. He aroused much rivalry, especially among the nobility, and on 4 August 1265 he was trapped on the low ground of the lower Avon valley, between forces from the Welsh border county on the one hand and the royal army headed by Prince Edward, a much sterner warrior than his father, on the other.

The battle took place north of Evesham and resulted in a decisive victory for the royal army. It is reported that casualties were very high indeed. They included Simon de Montfort himself, who was hacked to death on the battlefield, and also, according to contemporary chroniclers, about 160 of his supporting knights. The victory ensured that Edward would eventually succeed to the throne, bringing a reign of strong rule and military conquest, but Simon de Montfort, 'that knight so true' according to a popular ballad, was widely mourned, and became a folk hero to later generations.

Chapter 6

Development, Change and Contention:
the Tudors and early Stuarts, 1485-1642

The firm rule of Henry VII brought comparative stability to Worcestershire, as it did to the rest of the country. The reign came at the start of a period of rising population and increased production, so that by 1642 there were many more people in England than in 1485. These were also years of change and contention, which saw the final break-up of medieval society and which were disrupted by acute religious and political controversies.

Population and plague

The population of Worcestershire may well have doubled during this period. Estimates for the first 80 years are difficult to make but the Bishop's Census taken in 1563 gives the number of families in each parish for the greater part of the county. Assuming an average family size of 4.5—for many households had servants and relatives as well as parents and children—the population of Worcestershire may have been about 37,000 in 1563, while that of the city of Worcester was about 4,250. The study of parish registers, which survive for several parishes from 1538, suggests that by 1642 there were some 80,000 people in the county, about a fifth of the number living there today. A survey made in Worcester in 1646 confirms that the city's population was then about 8,000, barely a tenth of the 1981 total.

In most parishes there were more baptisms than burials, except in exceptional plague years, when the number of burials could be several times the average. The Harewell triptych in Besford church, erected about 1594, displays the emblems of death as a warning of the brevity of life. An inscription reminds the living that: 'The sounds the woeful watche when death with dreadful stroke Returns all flesh to mouldie earth'.

At Ribbesford there were 188 burials in 1593, nearly three times the average for the decade. Contemporaries saw such visitations as the hand of God. The vicar of Ribbesford wrote in the register this salutory text: 'Geve no occasion of Evell but fear Gods Anger'.

Scholars have noted, however, that epidemics usually followed a run of bad harvests, as in 1558. They often came after a rise of population, either by natural increase or by immigration, and can be interpreted as 'readjustment to a proper balance' between food production and consumption.

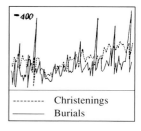

---------- Christenings
—— Burials

58 *The number of annual baptisms and burials in six Worcester parishes, 1540-1639*

Farming

The yield of the annual harvest was a prime concern to everyone. The south-east was still the best farming area. Here a four-course rotation was usual, as at Norton Beauchamp where two large open fields were described in 1585 as '... divided into four parts according to the course of husbandry, for 3 crops of corn to be had and taken thereof and the foarth to be yearly fallow ...'. The three crops were wheat, barley and a legume (peas/beans/pulses or vetches). They were part of a mixed farming system, with cattle and sheep eating some of the corn and giving manure to the land. Animals were kept in large pastures and grazed the open fields after harvest.

Around Evesham the tradition of growing fruit and vegetables continued. Most of the producers were small-holders, who got their livelihood from labour-intensive crops. Apples and pears were the most important fruits and a contemporary wrote: 'Worcestershire is a pleasant, fruitful and rich county ... every hedge and highway beset with fruit, but especially with pears, whereof they make that pleasant drink called perry ... bolder than any you tasted in London'. In the early 17th century the mild climate encouraged the growing of tobacco, newly imported from Virginia, but this was illegal, and in 1627 growers from 14 parishes were presented to the Quarter Sessions. Hops were another Worcestershire speciality, especially in the Teme valley.

Elsewhere, farming was more pastoral, especially on the peripheral uplands, where rye was more easily grown than wheat. Changes were made to increase food supply and new land was cultivated, as on Malvern Chase. In Yardley and district the proportion of farmland under crops rose after 1610 from a third to a half. Many farmers produced large surpluses of cheese, as at Alvechurch, where yeoman John Anger had 208 cheeses in 1598. The need for more food was greatest in the far north, where the expanding metal trades attracted many immigrants. In Belbroughton and Chaddesley Corbett a stock rearing economy was replaced after 1600 by a mixture of corn and sheep, and there was greater use of the commons.

Manufacturing

59 *A farm labourer*

As well as the artisan-retailers found in all towns and some villages, specialised manufactures developed rapidly in favoured areas. Foremost of these was the manufacture of cloth. In 1540 John Leland wrote that: 'the wealthe of the Towne of Worcester standeth most by Drapering'. He also noted 'clothinge' at Bromsgrove and Kidderminster. Droitwich and Evesham were other important centres, and Bewdley was noted for its caps.

Some of the wool came from within the county but that of best quality was from Shropshire and Herefordshire. Cloth-making involved many skills which were generally undertaken by independent artisans of moderate means, though a few became very wealthy. Much of the spinning was contracted out to home workers, though a few wealthy clothiers had employees working in 'spinning chambers'. Weavers ranged from small operators with a single loom to rich clothiers who also marketed the finished product. Between these extremes were men like Henrie Wheeler (d.1615), who lived in part of the timber-framed building which still stands at 40-42 Friar Street in Worcester. Woven cloth was sent to a fuller to be thickened, sheared and cleaned, and sometimes to a dyer for colouring. The 'teynter yards' where cloth was stretched on racks to dry after fulling or dying were a familiar sight on the outskirts of all cloth-making towns, as on the site of the former Black Friars in Worcester. The wealthiest tradesmen were the clothiers, who sold cloth as well as making it. A few attained enormous wealth, for example Thomas Wilde of Worcester (d.1610), whose goods were worth over £700 and who converted the medieval Commandery into a 31-room mansion.

Metal-working was also of more than local importance. It was based on the iron-bearing Carboniferous rocks of south Staffordshire but embraced a number of north Worcestershire parishes. These are shown on Fig. 61. The relatively poor farming of this upland area and the lack of restrictions by manorial lords, trade guilds and other vested interests helped the metal trades to develop. Technical innovations included the water-powered blast furnace, introduced about 1560, and the slitting mill, used after 1600 to cut bar iron into rods. 'Dud' Dudley, brought home in 1619 to manage his father's ironworks, even patented the smelting of iron ore with coal in the hope of checking the loss of wood for charcoal, but jealous ironmasters prevented its adoption.

Nails, needles and scythes were the specialised products. As early as 1538 nails for Nonsuch Palace in Surrey were bought from Reynolde Warde of Dudley. Redditch was the chief centre for needles, while scythe-making was concentrated around the Clent Hills, where fast-flowing streams provided water power. In all these trades the family was the chief unit of production and metal-working was often combined with farming. Scythe-making needed most skill and its practitioners were often wealthy yeomen. In May 1605, at the end of the scyth-making season, Richard Pugh of Belbroughton had 'sithes redye wroughte' valued at £100 and 'yron and Steele unbwrought' worth £9. Nailers were usually much poorer, for example Roger White of Dudley, who died in 1558/9. His goods were worth only £3 8s., which included tools and stock, as well as debts for 'Iren nayles'.

Marketing

As previously, the products of field and workshop were exchanged at bustling weekly markets and at the annual fairs. In Bewdley, at the fairs of St George (23 April) and St Andrew (30 November), stallholders crowded into the market-place and 'standings' were set aside for 'the pewterers' and other travelling chapmen. One such chapman was Robert Clarke from Yorkshire, who sold knives bought in Sheffield. He happened to die in Worcester in the winter of 1580-81 and the debts on his inventory show him dealing with local cutlers and ironmongers on a circuitous route through Worcestershire and east Herefordshire.

Greater availability of a wide range of consumer goods is a feature of this period. In the larger towns, fashionable fabrics and other luxury items were sold by the mercers, some of whom were men of great wealth. Richard Harewood of Worcester (d.1583) had cloths worth £116, including satins, silks and velvets. Mercers also sold spices, dried fruits and sugar. Peter Gough (d.1573) had an apothecary's department, and the list of his drugs and potions is a document over eight feet long.

60 A mercer's shop, with hats, hose and other wares displayed on rails

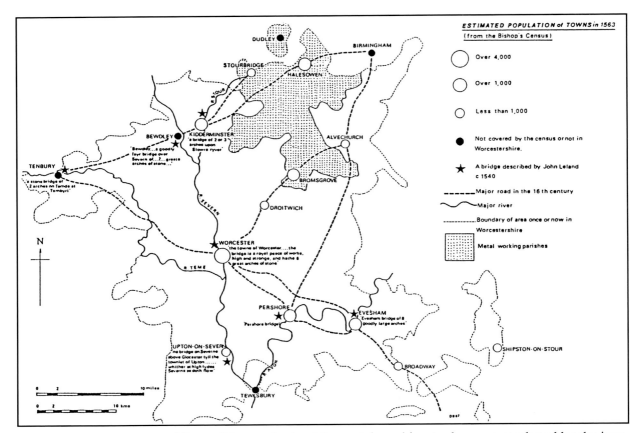

61 The towns, roads and bridges of rural Worcestershire, showing the parishes where metal-working trades were important

Many of the products of the metal-working trades were marketed by the iron-masters, who also organised much of the production. Among them were Edward Foley of Stourbridge and his son Richard (1580-1657), who had 19 furnaces and forges in the Stour valley and elsewhere by 1636. The Foleys had a warehouse at Bewdley and the Gloucester port books record increasing quantities of iron goods being taken downstream. Upstream cargoes included high quality ores from south Wales and the Forest of Dean.

Dissolution of the monasteries

This event was particularly dramatic in Worcestershire, where there were so many religious houses. Their wealth aroused much envy, Worcester Priory alone having an annual income of £1,385 9s. 9d. in 1535. Abuses were often described and sometimes exaggerated. At Halesowen one abbot was ordered to remove 'evil women'! In 1536 a monk at Pershore complained that his fellows drank and bowled 'after collacyon until 10 or 12 of the clock' and came to matins next morning 'as drunk as myss' (mice). Yet some monks were good and holy men, among them Clement Lichfield, the last but one Abbot of Evesham. Even the royal inquisitors called him 'a man chaste in his living', who 'right well overlooks the reparacions of his house'. In a final flourish of artistic energy, Lichfield built the campanile which still stands at Evesham. The most lavish late Perpendicular work in the county, however, is the chantry chapel of Prince Arthur, the King's eldest son, who was buried at Worcester in 1502.

By 1540 the surrender of all the houses had been received. Those who had been compliant received pensions. At Great Malvern for example, the prior, called 'an honest man' by his bishop, had £66 13s. 4d., and 10 monks had sums of £13 6s. 8d. or less. At Worcester, much of the Priory land was transferred to the new Chapter and the last prior became the first dean. In many cases, however, buildings were demolished with indecent haste. At Bordesley the Cistercian house was surrendered on 17 July and a fortnight later was described as 'defaced and plucked down'. When the authorised sale took place in September nearly all the glass and iron had been sold and the goods which could be found were worth only just over 70s.

Many of the monastic estates were sold to laymen. These were often loyal servants of the Crown, but rich merchants and successful lawyers were also eager for the status which land ownership conferred. To some, their new estates were investments and they never lived in the county themselves. The manors of Littleton, for example, were sold in 1557 to John Elliott, a 'citizen and merchant venturer of Bow Churchyard, London'; and later owners included two lord mayors of that city. Many new landowners, however, were prominent in the county. One of these was John Packington (1489-1551), a lawyer much favoured by Henry VIII. He acquired 30 Worcestershire manors, including Hampton Lovett, where he built 'a very goodly newe house of bricke', and the adjoining nunnery at Westwood, which he used as pasture for his horses. Another of his manors was Chaddesley Corbett, which passed to his nephew Humphrey Packington (1555-1631). Humphrey, according to Habington, 'seated himself at Harvington' in the west of that parish and built the fine brick hall which is now a major tourist attraction.

62 The detached bell tower at Evesham, built by Abbot Lichfield after 1513

The gentry

The Packingtons and others joined an elite of landed gentry at the apex of the county's social hierarchy. When the Heralds visited Worcestershire in 1569, they recognised 52 families as 'gentlemen' and confirmed their right to bear arms. Some of these came from well established aristocratic families, such as the Talbots at Grafton Manor. Others had risen from farming stock, for example the Lechmeres of Hanley Castle. Church monuments commemorate some members of this gentry class. One of the finest is that of Sir Thomas Bigg (d.1613) at Norton church. His mother had inherited the Norton estate from her brother, the diplomat Sir Philip Hoby (d.1558), who had acquired many Evesham Abbey manors. Sir Thomas and his Lady face each other across a prayer stool, with their nine children ranged as weepers below. A different kind of monument is the superb semi-reclining effigy of Thomas 1st Lord Coventry (d.1639) at Croome D'Abitot. He was Lord Keeper of the Great Seal and the carving has been attributed to Nicholas Stone.

Initiatives for clearing land and developing new technologies often came from the gentry. The Russells bought the buildings and lands of Little Malvern Priory, which included the brackened slopes of the Malvern Hills. Their library included

63 Humphrey Packington (1555-1631), the Worcestershire gentleman who rebuilt Harvington Hall

the treatise: 'The yder (idea) of burnying and dyggyng of ground for the tylling used in dyvers barren soiles to make them fruteful'. In August 1560 they had 59 cattle, 90 sheep and 28 swine, but by the summer of 1578 this had increased to 81 cattle, 220 sheep and 35 swine. Enterprise of another kind came from Sir William Sandys of Fladbury, who was granted a licence in 1635 to make the lower Avon navigable.

The gentry indulged themselves in new building, part of a nationwide process which has been called 'the great rebuild'. Eastington Hall at Longdon (c.1500) and Mere Hall at Hanbury (c.1560) are examples of timber-framed gentry houses, both with close studding as an expression of wealth. From 1540 brick was used for some of the grander houses, including Westwood Park and Grafton Manor. On the Cotswold fringe, stone was preferred, as at Woollas Hall, built for John Handford in 1611. Most Worcestershire great houses were traditional in plan. Symmetrical façades and other Renaissance features came late to the county, but the two-storey porch and the parlour window at Grafton Manor, added by John Talbot in 1587, are 'among the best things of that moment in England'.

64 *Memorial to Sir Thomas Bigg (d.1613) and his wife in St Egwin's church, Norton, near Evesham. Sir Thomas exemplifies the landowning gentry who were the leaders of rural communities*

Owners took great pride in their new houses and had an informed interest in their design. Sir Edward Pytts (1541-1618), Sheriff in 1612, commissioned a new house at Kyre Park in the north-west of the county. In 1588 he paid 40s. to John Symons of London 'for drawing my first platt for my house', but later his ideas changed and Symons was paid another £3 'for drawing my latter platt acording to my newe purpose'. Stone was brought down the Severn from Bewdley and then overland to Kyre. The carved chimney-pieces at Westwood and elsewhere, the plaster ceiling at The Nash, Kempsey, and the screen at Woollas Hall are a few of the many surviving fittings which reflect the good taste and wealth of their patrons.

Hangings of all kinds were used to cover internal walls, partly to reduce draughts, partly for decoration. These ranged from imported Flemish tapestries to painted canvas cloths worth only a few pence. One important workshop for tapestries was at Bordesley Abbey, established by William Sheldon (d.1570), squire of the nearby parish of Beoley. A few Sheldon tapestries are now exhibited in Birmingham but the most famous examples are the woven maps of Worcestershire, Oxfordshire and Berkshire and Gloucestershire, which are in the Victoria and Albert Museum.

65 *The interior of the chantry chapel in Worcester Cathedral, which was built to commemorate Prince Arthur, the eldest son of King Henry VII. He died in 1502, when only 16 years old, enabling his younger brother, later Henry VIII, to succeed to the throne in 1509. The tomb is a simple chest but there is a fine lierne vault ceiling and the reredos at the east end is crowded with figures and canopies*

66 *The Renaissance style porch and parlour window which were added to Grafton Manor in 1567*

Yeomen and husbandmen

In rural society, these formed the layer below the gentry. Technically, a yeoman was a freeholder and a husbandman a copyholder or leaseholder, but the terms were not used consistently. Yeomen were usually richer but in Worcestershire the husbandmen seem to have been more numerous.

A study of six pre-1550 inventories from Yardley gives a glimpse of the life-style of this group during the first part of the period. Rooms are listed on only one inventory, which shows two rooms: a chamber, used for sleeping, and a hall, used for everything else. William Harrison in his *Description of England* (1587), wrote that in his grandfather's time most people slept on the floor, 'lying on straw pallets', whereas servants often had only a single cover. The six Yardley households had a total of 11 mattresses or beds, but only one had a bedstead! There were between two and three sheets and two or three thicker covers per bed but in houses which were not draught-proof this was not excessive. Other furniture was sparse. Each house had a table board but only two had a cupboard—at that time merely a side table where articles could be placed. For storage there were two coffers, nearly two per house. The six inventories only produced one chair, one bench and four cushions but there must have been roughly hewn stools or forms not considered worth listing. Pewter utensils were plentiful, an average of 25 pieces per house, but other metals were sparse. The only real luxuries were the chafing-dishes owned by three households. These were portable grates which could be fitted with burning charcoal to keep food warm, the equivalent of modern hostess trolleys and must have been highly prized.

The many inventories which survive for the later part of the period show an improvement in living standards after 1550. Chimney stacks were inserted in many houses, often occupying the top bay of the hall so that the solar wing could be heated as well. Star-shaped chimney-stacks made of brick can often be seen protruding from timber-framed farm houses at this point. With smoke rising up a chimney, high open halls were no longer necessary and upper rooms were often inserted.

The inventory of Robert Leadon of Great Comberton (d.1614) shows a traditionally built house, with a kitchen and other service rooms at the lower end of the hall. At the upper end were the parlour (used as a sitting room as well as for sleeping), a ground-floor chamber (used just for sleeping), and a buttery. There were solars above the hall, the parlour and the chamber, but their primary purpose was for storage. The room over the hall contained onions and garlic as well as linen, malt, barley, wool and a cheese rack, indications of versatile farming.

Urban society

The towns had a parallel but different social structure to that of the countryside. William Harrison, in his *Description of England* (1587), distinguished 'the citizens or burgesses' from the poorer 'artificers or labourers'. 'The burgesses', he wrote, 'are free within the cities and are of some substance to beare office in the same.'

Most burgesses were master craftsmen, who had served an apprenticeship and were 'free' to practise their trade. They employed journeymen and had their own apprentices. Freelance labourers were another group. At Worcester they stood at the Grass Cross at the town centre with tools in their hands, ready to be hired if they had no work, by 5 a.m. in summer and 6 a.m. in winter.

Even in smaller towns the burgesses had some self-government. At Alvechurch the manorial courts were retained, but the burgesses had their own jury to deal with town affairs, and could elect their own bailiff each year. In the larger towns, there was almost complete self-government, usually by the richer burgesses. Charters recognised an inner group of aldermen and a larger group of councillors. In Worcester these were the twenty-four and forty-eight. Members were often related and formed a closely knit oligarchy. Analysis of the 1585 Lay Subsidy shows that 19 of the 29 most heavily taxed citizens were on the twenty-four. At Evesham, town affairs were closely monitored by the abbot but self-government grew after the Dissolution and the charter of 1605 recognised 'the 12 and 12'. At Kidderminster there had been a '12 and 24' since the Middle Ages, but this became 'the 12 and 25' when the town was belatedly incorporated in 1636.

Like their gentry and yeoman cousins in the countryside, the richer burgesses built new houses, especially after 1560. The earlier type of town house is represented by the 'Merchants House' from Bromsgrove, which is now at the Avoncroft Museum of Buildings. This had an open hall with a louvre outlet for the smoke, and a storied cross wing at the upper end. It was built about 1485 and became the home of Richard Lylley (d.1558), a prosperous dyer. Later town houses had fireplaces and chimney-stacks, were often richly decorated, and could be three or more stories high, for restricted sites necessitated upwards rather than sideways growth. The Bailiff's House, Bewdley, built in 1610, is an example of this type, and six other Bewdley houses have inscribed dates between 1600 and 1642.

Less is known about the employees of men like Richard Lylley. The surviving inventories of Worcester labourers show that most had goods valued between £2 and £6 and lived in homes of one or at most two rooms, often with only the most rudimentary furniture and utensils.

67 The Bailiff's House at Bewdley, dated 1610

The Poor

In both town and country, 'the poor' were a persistent social problem. At Worcester, a survey in 1557 gave a total of 734 'blind, lame, impotent, sick and those unable to get their livings'. This was about a fifth of the city's population, and the proportion was perhaps higher in later years. Many were widows, often living alone. A distinction was made between the deserving poor, who were generally dealt with sympathetically, and the vagrants and beggars who were treated harshly.

The plight of some of the homeless unemployed is illustrated by the petition of William Dench of Longdon, labourer, made to the Quarter Sessions in 1617. Since 1612, with the consent of the Overseers of the parish but without licence of the lord of the manor, he, his wife and seven small children had dwelt 'in a Sheepcot given to him and his family' by a local yeoman. His petition was simply for licence to stay!

Some deserving poor were admitted to almshouses, such as those still standing at Hanley Castle. Gifts to the poor were commonplace. There were bequests of this

68 A family of vagabonds. These homeless and unemployed people were a major social problem

69 *A Tudor grammar school, showing a schoolmaster, his birch and his pupils*

70 *One of the garderobes at Harvington, with a trap-door leading to a priest's hole*

kind in 24 of the Bewdley wills proved between 1545 and 1642. Most were to 'the poor mens box' or simply to 'the poor', but Anne Rushbury (d.1614) left 30s. 'to the poor people of Bewdley, wherein my poor washerwoman shall be best rewarded above others'.

Education

The county was well provided with grammar schools, which taught Latin and Greek to a wide social range of boys, including the sons of gentry. Petty schools taught a smattering of reading and writing but many boys and nearly all girls went without any formal education. Nevertheless, there is evidence of improving literacy, especially in Worcester.

The grammar schools are well documented. At least nine chantry schools survived the Reformation, though some were refounded under other names, for example King Edward VI School, Stourbridge (1552). By 1642 there were about 20 such schools, most of them in the towns, but some in smaller places such as Powick and Wolverley. The latter was endowed by William Seabright of London, Esq., who gave two houses and 20 acres of land in Bethnal Green to erect 'a free grammar school for the children of the parish where I was bredd up'. Some boys went on to the universities or to the Inns of Court, but to many the strictly classical education was of little relevance in later life. The vocational training given to apprentices was an important part of the educational system. Most seem to have been well treated, though in 1566 the authorities protected a glover's apprentice in Worcester from 'unlawful correction' and 'an inadequate diet'.

Law and order

A wrong-doer in Tudor Worcestershire could come before any one of a jumble of courts. The Council of the Marches, which was based at Ludlow Castle in Shropshire, had jurisdiction over the county and often met at Bewdley. Twice a year Assize judges visited the county town, then on the Midland circuit. Four times a year local Justices of the Peace, drawn from the gentry, sat at Quarter Sessions, which dealt with many criminal offences, as well as with the Poor Law and other administration. Some towns had their own courts of Record. Moral offences went to the Church courts while serious civil issues were heard in London, sometimes before the hated Star Chamber.

The records of the Quarter Sessions give a glimpse of crime between 1591 and 1642. Larceny and assault were the most common offences. In 1623 Frances Howlder of Salwarpe, spinster, was presented for stealing a hen worth 6d. A greater threat to society came from John Guest of Bromsgrove in 1617, who beat up several neighbours and 'tore the clothes' from the back of the local constable. Cases of forcible entry included offences against game, as in 1599 when two men were hunting the deer in Bordesley Park using cross-bows and arrows. Other offences were sheltering rogues and keeping an unlicensed alehouse. In 1620 Anthony Barnes of Wick was indicted for suffering rogues 'usually to lodge in his barn', and John Huntbach of Stourbridge for 'keeping a house of game with cards and ... shovel board'. In 1623 three men of Fladbury 'kept tippling houses without licences and sold beer therein'. Cases of slander were also common. In 1613 Eleanor Wheeler and Joyce Gould of Stoulton were charged with 'maliciously rumouring' that the vicar's wife had poisoned her former husband. It was shown that Eleanor 'hath been a great source of discord between man and wife' while Joyce was 'a wandering woman going from house to house from town to town ...'.

Various local officials helped the Justices to keep the peace. The most important was the constable. In most parishes he was appointed at the Easter vestry meeting but in towns he was chosen by the Corporation. At Worcester there were two constables for each of the six wards, and from 1597 they were reinforced by a night watch of eight men who patrolled from 9 p.m. to 5 a.m.

Punishments were still savage, though perhaps a little less so than in the Middle Ages. Executions were carried out in public places like Red Hill, Worcester. All parishes had their stocks and whipping post and in places these still remain, as at the west end of the church at Rock. At Bewdley administrators' accounts have payments 'for mendying of the pillory', for 'hynges for the pryson door' and for 'setting up the gomble stoole', this being the ducking apparatus often used for scolds.

71 *An early 17th-century witch, with a raven as her familiar*

Supernatural beliefs

Though there was discord in Worcestershire over religious practices, nearly everyone shared basic assumptions about the existence of God and the necessity for worship. There were occasional sceptics, like Thomas Aston of Ribbesford, who claimed in 1616 that 'the word of God is but man's invention', but such incidents were rare.

Belief in God was part of a wider belief in supernatural forces. A modern historian has written:'Most men and women ... still lived in a world of magic, in which God and the devil intervened daily, a world of witches, fairies and charms'. This underlay the faith in 'cunning men' or wizards, the popularity of astrology and the occasional outbreak of witch-hunting. In 1549 an accused sorcerer argued 'there be within England about 500 conjurers', and named Worcestershire as one of four counties where they were most numerous. When Richard Baxter came to Kidderminster in 1641, he found some people believing that 'Christ was the Sun and the Holy Ghost the Moon'. After Diana Hewes of Bromsgrove had beaten off an assailant in 1617, he feared she would bewitch him or set fire to his house.

The Church before the Reformation

Until the 1540s or later, most Worcestershire people retained medieval beliefs and practices. Many wills have preambles like that of William Hill of Bewdley, tanner (d.1535), who committed his soul 'to Allmyghty God to oure blessed lady hys mother and to all the saynts in heven'. Church rebuilding and extension continued, in parish churches as well as in the monasteries. At Rock, for example, the tower and the south aisle were added to the Norman church in 1510 by the local squire, Sir Humphrey Conynsby. The diocese lacked spiritual leadership at this time, however, for until 1535 the bishopric was used to reward faithful servants of the Crown, four of them being Italian diplomats in Rome!

This was a conservative area but there were some stirrings for reform. In the 1520s images on the High Cross at Worcester were defaced by early Lutherans. John Ashe, parson of Staunton, was one extreme reformer and in 1536 was

*72 John Whitgift,
Bishop of Worcester
1577-83, and later
Archbishop of
Canterbury*

accused of attacking the bishop and the king as well as the Abbot of Evesham. Hugh Latimer, appointed bishop in 1535, preached a much quoted sermon against relics, claiming that they 'deluded the people'. He left Worcester in 1539 and was later burned for heresy by Mary Tudor. His successor, Nicholas Heath, was less zealous, and resigned in 1552, declining to accept the new prayer-book; but he was reinstated under Mary and later became Archbishop of York.

The Reformation

The acts for the Dissolution of Chantries in 1545 and 1547 and for the use of the new *Book of Common Prayer* in 1549 and 1552 made a great impact on the appearance and worship of every parish church. Roods were removed, chantry chapels were demolished and wall paintings were whitewashed. Some things were replaced during Mary's reign between 1553 and 1558 but the Elizabethan settlement of 1559 finally established the Church of England. It was seen as the *via media anglicana* between traditional Roman Catholicism on one hand and the extreme Reformers on the other, the latter now being known as Puritans.

At diocesan level, successive bishops of Worcester had the difficult task of holding this broad Church together. The most able was probably John Whitgift, Bishop 1577-83, and then Archbishop of Canterbury. He was 'a stern disciplinarian', who upheld some unity in spite of 'stubborn Papists and contentious Protestants'. The longest episcopacy was that of John Thornborough, 1616-42. He had to deal with the high church reforms of Archbishop Laud and the opposition they provoked from puritans.

When in the diocese the bishops lived regally in the Palace at Hartlebury. Inventories show that the Dean and Chapter also enjoyed good living standards. Canon Backhouse (d.1586) had goods worth £580; his rooms in the cathedral close were richly furnished with pictures, maps and hangings; and he had a small farm in the country. He was a man of some learning, for his books, worth £20, included works by Calvin, Hooker and Luther. In contrast, the parish clergy were often ignorant and nearly always poor. Only 19 per cent of them were graduates in 1560, though this rose to 52 per cent by 1620. The tithes of many parishes had been held by the monasteries and were now transferred to laymen. The right to marry added to the financial burden. Edmund Rea, Vicar of Great Malvern, 1612-40, had a stipend of only 'VII pounds by the yere', plus a house and garden. Fortunately, he had a private income, and in his will left £100 as a stock to increase the income of his successors.

Roman Catholics

These were the greatest threat to Church unity in Worcestershire in the 16th century. In 1577 Bishop Whitgift found that Mass was said 'at various houses', that priests had come 'from beyond the seas' and that men were buried at night 'because they would not receive the service now being used'. Two priests were captured in the county in 1581, the year when the fines for recusancy were greatly increased. The Babington plot to put Mary Queen of Scots on the throne, which was discovered in 1586, and the threat of the Spanish Armada in 1588 intensified the persecution of the Roman Catholics.

Those who declined to attend the parish church were called recusants. In 1593 there were 180 such recusants in 40 Worcestershire parishes, most of them Roman Catholics. Several came from gentry families and this stiffened the movement in the county. The Habingtons of Hindlip, the Lyttletons of Hagley, the Packingtons of Harvington, the Talbot's of Grafton, the Windsors of Hewell Grange and the Wintours of Huddington were among 'the better sorte' of recusants. Some great houses still have authentic priest holes and roof chapels, as at Harvington.

The Gunpowder Plot

One such house, Huddington Court near Droitwich, was the hub of the notorious Gunpowder Plot, the conspiracy among Roman Catholics to blow up the Houses of Parliament in the autumn of 1605. It was hoped that the king and his ministers would be killed and that the Catholics could seize power in the resulting confusion. The instigator seems to have been Robert Catesby of Northampton, a relative of the Throckmortons of Coughton Court just across the Warwickshire border, but a majority of the plotters were Worcestershire gentlemen.

The first details of the plot were worked out at Huddington, the home of Robert Wintour and his brothers. A former soldier, Guy Fawkes, was engaged to light the gunpowder hidden in the cellars below Parliament but on

73 Huddington Court, a timber-framed house of the early 16th century, much modified in the 1580s. This was the home of the Wintour family, which was deeply involved in the Gunpowder Plot of 1605

5 November he was arrested and the plot exposed. The conspirators, a dejected band of about 30 mounted men, came to Huddington on 6 November, knowing that capture would mean torture and cruel death. After a short sleep they assembled for Mass at 3 a.m. and then left for Wales in the faint hope of raising Catholic support. The riders eventually reached Holbeach House on the edge of Staffordshire at 10 p.m., after 16 hours on roads made almost impassable by heavy rain. But here they were overtaken by a posse of about two hundred men led by the Sheriff of Worcestershire, Sir Richard Walsh of Shelsey Walsh. Some of the plotters were killed and others taken but Robert Wintour was one who escaped and found refuge at Hagley. After some weeks, however, he was betrayed by the cook and was taken to London. In due course, 14 of the conspirators were hung, drawn and quartered, some of them at Worcester.

Other Catholic houses were searched, including Hindlip House, the home of Thomas Habington. After days of destruction, four men were found, one of them Nicholas Owen, the ingenious designer of many hiding places. All four were executed but Habington himself was spared, on condition that he stayed in Worcestershire for the rest of his life. This was probably on the intervention of his brother-in-law, Lord Mounteagle, who is reputed to have warned the Government of the plot after receiving a letter telling him not to attend Parliament on 5 November.

Puritans

Their presence was increasingly felt, especially in the towns. Puritanism was rooted in the Bible, which figured more often in inventories as English translations became available. There was greater stress on preaching than on ritual, and high moral standards were urged. One well-known Puritan was Edward Winslow of Droitwich (1594-1655). He was apprenticed to a London printer in 1613 but later went to Amsterdam and then sailed for New England with the Pilgrim Fathers in 1620. Winslow Street in New Plymouth, Massachusetts, still bears his name.

The Puritans emphasised Sabbath observance. In 1617 William Jeffries of Longdon petitioned against 'sports and morrices and dancings on the Sabbath days'. A well-known case concerned Gerard Prior, Vicar of Eldersfield, who preached a sermon against profaning the Sabbath and was indiscreet enough to pray publicly that the king 'might be delivered from profanness, vanity and popery'.

74 Richard Baxter (1613-91), a Puritan divine who became lecturer at Kidderminster in 1641

Regard for good preaching led many towns to appoint a lecturer, beginning at Worcester in 1589. At first he was paid £10 but by 1628 this had risen to £40, much more than the sum received by most parish clergy. The preference of the leading citizens for the lecturer's sermons rather than the cathedral services caused dissension, especially after the appointment of Roger Mainwaring as dean in 1634. Mainwaring introduced many Laudian reforms, including the use of high Anglican vestments and the erection of a marble altar. One notable lecturer in the county was Richard Baxter, appointed at Kidderminster in 1641. His preaching had much to do with the growth of nonconformity in north Worcestershire as a continuing form of the Puritan tradition.

Chapter 7

The Civil Wars and Commonwealth, 1642-1660

The county's role during a time of crisis

Historians differ about the causes of the Civil War but agree that this was a time of constitutional crisis. Some contemporaries saw it as a struggle for power between the King and the Court on the one hand and Parliament on the other. For others, religious differences were fundamental. Today, most scholars argue that economic factors and the role of the land-owning gentry must also be considered.

Most of the fighting took place during the First Civil War, from 1642 to 1646. There was further conflict during the Second Civil War in 1647 and 1648, leading to the execution of King Charles I on 30 January 1649. As the Parliamentary extremists tried to consolidate their power, the Scots and others recognised the eldest son of the dead king as Charles II, but a military campaign to restore the monarchy led to defeat at the Battle of Worcester on 3 September 1651. In one of the great romances of history, the young claimant to the throne was able to escape to France, but there were nearly nine years of Commonwealth rule before he was restored as King Charles II on 12 May 1660.

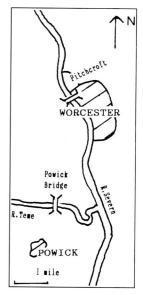

75 *The sites of the Battle of Powick Bridge, 1642, and the Battle of Worcester 1651*

Throughout, Worcestershire played a crucial strategic role. Much of Parliament's support was in the south-east, especially in London, whereas the Royalists were strongest in outlying regions such as Wales. Routes from both these areas converged in Worcestershire, and Bewdley, Worcester and Upton-on-Severn were all nodal crossing points of the Severn. The north of the county, with its metal trades, was an important source of arms, shot being produced in Stourbridge and cannon in Dudley. With the Parliamentarians controlling the arsenals at Portsmouth, Hull and London, it was vital for the Royalists to have these alternative supplies.

It has been well said that 'the English Civil war was not a war of rigid fronts, mass armies and solidly occupied territories ... it was a war within a community, in which there was substantial support for both sides in most parts of the country'. Worcestershire was predominantly a Royalist county; there were strong Parliamentary minorities, especially in the towns. Of the aristocrats and the landed gentry, who had great influence over their tenantry, the majority were for the king, but even here Parliament had its adherents, such as the Lechmeres of Hanley Castle and the Lygons of Madresfield.

Because of the county's strategic importance, armies marched and rode across it, plundering as they went. In the last years of the First Civil War, local farmers and labourers formed bands of 'Club men' to resist this process. Great damage was done to crops and to roads, while bridges were broken to hold up pursuers. Because

*76 Important places
in Worcestershire
during the Civil Wars
of 1642-1651*

of the impossibility of controlling wide tracts of country with forces of limited size, both sides concentrated on garrisoning the main towns and other defensible places. From these, raiding parties would harass enemy troops or try to raise a siege elsewhere. For most of the war, the Royalists held garrisons at Worcester, Dudley and Hartlebury, but the Parliamentarians kept control of Gloucester, not very far beyond the county boundary.

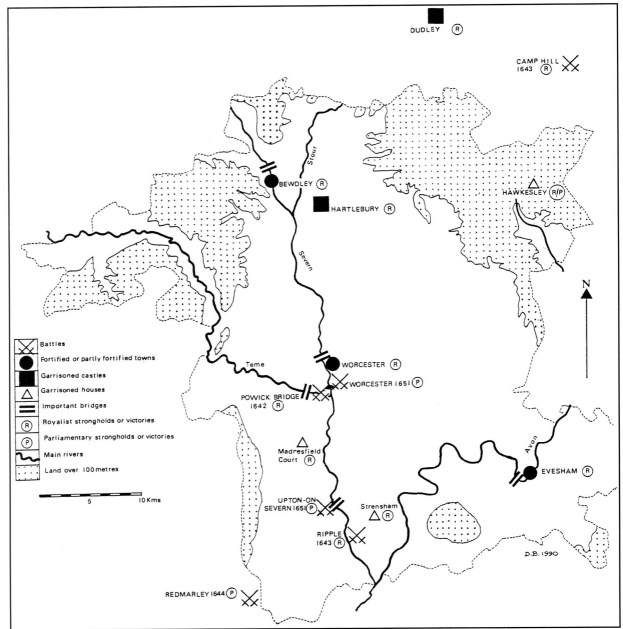

DUDLEY Ⓡ

CAMP HILL 1643 Ⓡ

BEWDLEY Ⓡ

HARTLEBURY Ⓡ

HAWKESLEY Ⓡ/Ⓟ

WORCESTER Ⓡ

WORCESTER 1651 Ⓟ

POWICK BRIDGE 1642 Ⓡ

MADRESFIELD COURT Ⓡ

EVESHAM Ⓡ

UPTON-ON-SEVERN 1651 Ⓟ

STRENSHAM Ⓡ

RIPPLE 1643 Ⓡ

REDMARLEY 1644 Ⓟ

D.B. 1990

✕✕	Battles
●	Fortified or partly fortified towns
■	Garrisoned castles
△	Garrisoned houses
=	Important bridges
Ⓡ	Royalist strongholds or victories
Ⓟ	Parliamentary strongholds or victories
∿	Main rivers
⋯	Land over 100 metres

5   10 Kms

The action at Powick Bridge, 23 September 1642

The king raised his standard at Nottingham on 22 August 1642. His aim was to advance on London, but, in the hope of recruiting more soldiers in Wales and the Welsh borders, he came south to Shrewsbury. The Parliamentarians, led by the Earl of Essex, marched from London to intercept him. Meanwhile, a baggage train captained by Sir John Bryan was taking plate and supplies to the king. Essex sent troops under Colonel John Brown, a Scots professional soldier, to detain it at Worcester. At Powick Bridge, just south of Worcester, these troops were intercepted by Royalist cavalry led by the king's nephew, Prince Rupert, already famous for his exploits in the Rhineland and elsewhere.

The skirmish was a fierce one, but it happened almost by chance, when a small detachment of the Parliamentarians, led by Colonel Sandys, rode over Powick Bridge and up a lane towards Worcester. They were fired at by sentries, posted by Rupert whilst his troopers recovered from their long ride to Worcester in a field beside the lane. Sandys needed time to rally his men and bring up reinforcements but Rupert, though not expecting battle, acted very quickly, and ordered his men to charge, even though their armour was unbuckled and they were not in formation. This quick response carried the day, and there was dreadful carnage in the congested lane leading back to the bridge. Some men were trampled to death while others drowned in the River Teme, and the depleted force had to retire in disorder, eventually rejoining the main army at Pershore.

In spite of victory, the outnumbered Royalists retired towards Shrewsbury, leaving the way clear for Essex to occupy Worcester. A number of indignities occurred, including the desecration of the cathedral. 'The city is so vile, it resembles Sodom', wrote one Parliamentary fanatic. But as Charles marched from Shropshire towards London, Essex left Worcester to cut him off at Edgehill in Oxfordshire, the first great battle of the war, leaving Worcester as a Royalist stronghold until 1646.

Fortifications

It was imperative for the Royalist cause that Worcester should be retained, and no expense was spared to defend it. The medieval stone walls of Worcester had not been designed to resist 17th-century cannon. In any case they were in poor repair, though the seven gates were still solid enough to be closed at night. As shown on Fig. 76, the walls were strengthened by a number of bastions, where packed earth was enclosed by stone walls. Much the most impressive of the new fortifications was Fort Royal, built to command the London road and to secure the high ground of Red Hill. A line of earthworks connected Fort Royal to the old walls just south of Friar's gate. Another line ran from the fort to the River Severn, thereby enclosing Castle Hill, the site of the Norman castle, where new gun emplacements were mounted. To the west the river provided protection, but a hexagonal bastion served as a bridgehead on the far side of the Severn bridge.

Earthworks were erected at Evesham and there were some fortifications at Bewdley, probably a strengthening of the gates. The strongest defensive point was Dudley, with its castle still standing on its superb defensive site. Hartlebury Castle was another strong point and a number of country houses were fortified for the war.

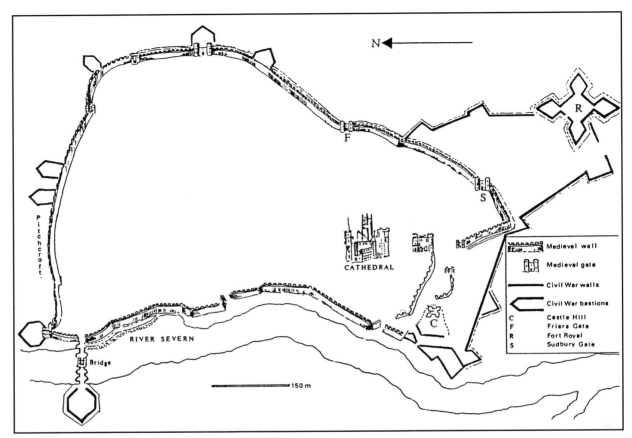

77 *Fortifications of Worcester in the 1640s and in 1651*

Battles, marches and sieges

Some of the fiercest action in Worcestershire occurred in the south-west, part of an ongoing strategic stuggle for the lower Severn valley. Early in 1643 Prince Maurice, the inexperienced younger brother of Rupert, took up the Royalist command in Worcestershire, and at once marched to the south-west to counter an expedition northwards from Gloucester by Sir William Waller, at that time the best Parliamentarian general. Largely due to bold cavalry movements, Maurice defeated Waller at Ripple and succeeded in securing Upton-on-Severn bridge. In 1643, however, the Royalist hold on this part of the county began to weaken. Upton-on-Severn bridge was lost and a force of Royalists, led by Colonel Nicholas Mynne, who had learnt his fighting in Ireland, was heavily defeated by Parliamentarians led by Edward Massey, now Governor of Gloucester. Those killed included Colonel Mynne, whose body was taken into Gloucester and buried with dignity, showing a chivalrous side to this war which was picked up in his contemporary epitaph: 'He was missed by his friends, honoured by his foes ... being the shrewdest enemy in Christendom ...'.

Other actions resulted from military marches through the county. In 1643 the Parliamentarians failed to check Rupert at Camp Hill, in the far north of King's Norton, as he marched towards Birmingham. In May 1644 the king himself zigzagged about the county, finally breaking down the bridge at Pershore to avoid pursuers led by Waller. A month later he was chased north-west as far as Bewdley but again avoided engagement. A sadder march was that in 1645, after the king's defeat at the Battle of Naseby in Leicestershire, thought by many to have been the turning point of the war. He stayed two days in Bewdley at *The Angel*, but on his way there had buried at Kidderminster 'a woman wounded at the battle in Leicestershire'.

There were engagements and actions of other kinds. In May 1643 Waller got as far into the county as the outskirts of Worcester but was chased away by a relieving force from Oxford, the Royal headquarters. During June 1643 a Parliamentary force under Lord Denbigh besieged Dudley and beat off relieving troops, though eventually they had to abandon the siege. In May 1645 Massey captured Evesham for Parliament in a brilliant attack which saw heavy fighting on the improvised ramparts. The most daring scoop of the war in Worcestershire occurred late in 1644 when 'Tinker' Fox, a man who has been described as 'a typical specimen of a fighting Puritan', carried out a daring commando-type raid on Bewdley, seizing the governor and lodging him in the Tower of London.

During the first half of 1646 the Royalist cause continued to deteriorate. The garrisons at Dudley and Hartlebury surrendered and so eventually did the city of Worcester, which was besieged from 21 May until terms were agreed on 19 June, leading to surrender four days later. The final morning of the siege was a time of pathos, with the Royalist officers and gentlemen holding a service in the cathedral at 6 a.m., the end of Anglican worship there for 14 years. They then marched out of the gates for disarming, when the leaders of Royalist society in the county—men like the Earl of Shrewsbury of Grafton, Henry Townshend of Elmley Lovett and Sir William Russell of Strensham—had to swear formally never again to bear arms against Parliament.

The last Royalist rising and the Battle of Worcester, 1651

After five politically active years—which saw various shifts of alliances and the execution of Charles I—war returned to Worcestershire in August 1651, as an army of Scots, headed by the young Charles II, marched into the county from the north with about 16,000 men, hoping to join forces from Wales. With most people weary of war, his reception along the way was far from rapturous, but he was received into Worcester, for this reason later known as 'the faithful City'.

A much larger force was approaching through Evesham, under the command of Oliver Cromwell, the successful Parliamentary general who was now Lord Protector. As in earlier years, there was sharp fighting by small detachments to secure Upton-on-Severn, which was taken for Cromwell after heroic actions on both sides. The bridge was quickly repaired and a large Parliamentary force crossed to the west bank, cutting off the Scots from relief from Wales. Morale among the Parliamentarians was high, a contemporary noting that as Cromwell passed 'from one guard or regiment to another, he was received with abundance of joy and extraordinary shouting'.

Cromwell planned to catch the Scots in a pincer movement, with an attack on Worcester each side of the Severn. His main force formed a crescent south-east of the city, where he was opposed by troops under the Scots Commander, the Duke

78 A pikeman, from Jacob de Gheyn's drillbook, The Exercise of Arms, *published at The Hague, 1607. He is bracing his pike against his foot and drawing his sword in preparation for receiving cavalry*

of Hamilton. The rest of Cromwell's forces, under General Fleetwood, came from Upton along the west bank of the Severn and formed up south of the River Teme, facing about half the Scots army, drawn up close to the 1642 battlefield. With two rivers crossing the likely battle area, Cromwell appreciated the importance of bridging points. He ordered boats to be collected and used them to build bridges, one over the Severn south of Worcester, the other over the Teme below Powick Bridge. The bridges were finished on 2 September and the attack from the south-west began early the next morning.

Preliminary fighting took place in and around Powick churchyard, where the marks of bullets can still be seen on the tower. As the Scots fell back, there was a fiercer struggle for the bridge, which the Scots were able to hold. Further east, the attackers crossed the Teme on the improvised bridge, but, as they tried a flanking movement towards the Scots at the bridge, they were held by doughty Highlanders under Major-General Pitscottie.

Cromwell, watching from the east bank, saw that the crisis of battle had come. More troops had to be sent in or his attack would be repulsed. Yet if he weakened his forces south-east of the city too much, the Scots would break out and assail the remnant. However, his superiority of numbers was such that he took the risk, and marched three brigades across the bridge of boats, so that they could charge the Highlanders. The Highlanders fought resolutely, but as officers and men fell, the survivors were driven back, retreat soon becoming a rout. Behind them, Powick bridge was taken and, as the Scots retreated, Cromwell's forces closed in on Worcester west of the Severn.

The Royalist commanders, who had watched these events from the top of the cathedral tower, perceived that their only hope was in counter-attack against Cromwell's weakened east bank forces. Two columns, led by Hamilton and Charles himself, gained some success, but the Royalist cavalry, kept back on Pitchcroft as a reserve, refused to support them, thus losing an opportunity to turn the tide of battle. Reacting quickly, Cromwell brought his brigades back over the Severn, and galloped to his broken centre, ordering his men first to stand firm and then to charge. This was one of the epic actions of history, with 'the saints of the Lord', as they liked to think of themselves, moving with terrible ferocity to storm the defences with hand-to-hand conflict. The cannon at Fort Royal were captured and turned on the city, so that great slaughter took place, as fugitives fought to get back through Sidbury Gate.

79 *Charles II, a contemporary portrait*

In the chaos, Charles himself was nearly cut down, but, according to legend, William Bagnall of Worcester used a team of oxen and their wagon to protect his monarch from avenging troopers. In the confusion, Charles was able to slip out of the city by the only gate which was open and escape along the Kidderminster Road. He left behind him not just defeat but annihilation, for of 16,000 men some 3,000 were dead and another 10,000 were prisoners, while the rest were fugitives or helpless wanderers. As perceived by the victors, 'the Lord of Hosts was wonderfully with us', and no-one could quarrel with Cromwell's own assessment that this was 'an absolute victory'.

Chapter 8

Restoration to Reform:
late Stuart and Georgian Worcestershire,
1660-1832

On 12 May 1660 the bridgewardens of Bewdley paid £6 3s. for 'wine and beare at the p(ro)clayminge the king'. There are similar records of bell ringing and toasts all over the county, though the increasing number of Worcestershire dissenters would not have shared the joy of their Royalist neighbours.

The Restoration did not bring immediate political stability to Worcestershire, as is shown by the displacement of dissenters and others from borough corporations in 1662, following the Act of Settlement and other legislation. It did begin a long period of economic growth and development, which culminated in the late 18th and early 19th centuries in what are commonly called the Agricultural and Industrial Revolutions. By 1831, a year before the Parliamentary Reform Act, the population of the county was 222,655, about four times the estimated total at the time of the Restoration.

80 *This seed and manure hopper, pulled by a horse, was one of many 18th-century inventions used on Worcestershire farms*

Population

Detailed studies of parish registers show that in most places population increased by about half between 1660 and 1750, but then doubled itself or more during the next 80 years. For a group of 12 parishes in north-east Worcestershire, including Alvechurch, Bromsgrove and Hanbury, the estimated totals are 5,828 in 1665 and 9,018 in 1750, with a known peak of 17,708 in 1831. The number of births per head of population was higher in the early 18th century than in the early 19th century, but the proportion of deaths showed a marked decline over the same period. For the 12 parishes, the number of burials per 1,000 people averaged 31 a year between 1700 and 1720, but between 1800 and 1820 the equivalent figure was only twenty-two. Epidemics still had catastrophic effects, as with the wave of smallpox from 1725 to 1729, when the burial rate in those parishes climbed to nearly 63, though afterwards there was a sudden increase of marriages and subsequently of baptisms.

The rates of increase were not constant throughout the county. In rural north-west Worcestershire the parishes in the deanery of Burford showed an increase between 1676 and 1801 of less than 100 per cent. On the other hand, the adjoining deanery of Kidderminster, which included many of the metal-working parishes on the edge of the south Staffordshire coalfield, had an increase of nearly 300 per cent. The city of Worcester rose from an estimated 4,000 in 1676 to 13,000 in 1801, and just over 23,000 in 1831.

Agriculture

The growth of population stimulated changes in agriculture, increasing the amount of food produced. New crops were introduced, open fields and waste areas were enclosed, and farming types were altered in response to market forces. Yet bad harvests could still cause abnormal burial rates, as between 1708 and 1712, or bring very high prices, as in 1800. The latter year was one of terrible scarcity, with the starving mob at Worcester attacking the city's bakers in a desperate attempt to obtain bread. There were good years also, as in the 1820s, when William Cobbett observed that 'the working people, especially near Worcester, seem to be better off than in many other parts'.

Improvements in farming technique were introduced by a small circle of gentry. Andrew Yarranton, from Astley, wrote a book in 1663 advocating the growth of clover as a means of fixing nitrogen in the soil, so increasing fertility. He claimed that this was particularly effective 'for gravelly, dry, sandy or rye land which is worn out with tillage and liming'. Another kind of improver was Thomas Foley, who invested some £500 in extensive water works at Chaddesley Corbett in the 1690s, transforming 'very poor arable land and sandy cony-warren' worth 5s. an acre into 'verdant meadows' worth over 20s. an acre.

The process of enclosure, under way in some areas since the Middle Ages, continued during this period. Much of it was by agreement between neighbours, but there were also Parliamentary Enclosure Acts, beginning with Malvern Chase in 1664. This process was especially frequent after 1750, as in 1765, when Worcestershire Acts included open lands in Bretforton, common fields in Lenchwick and Norton and in the borough of Evesham, and common meadows and wastes in Evenlode. In 1794 a report stated that in Worcestershire 'the lands are in general inclosed; there are, however, some considerable tracts in open fields'. A later report, in 1805, distinguished between 'ancient inclosure', where hedges were 'full of trees ... such as elm, willow, hazel, crabtree, hawthorn and fruit', and 'modern inclosures of post and rail or a quickset hedge'.

Arable farming remained important throughout the county, but was pre-eminent only in the south, though always with some livestock, particularly cattle. Wheat was the leading cereal. Farm inventories of Powick between 1676 and 1775 indicate that 67 per cent of cultivated land supported wheat, as against 27 per cent for pulses and six per cent for barley. Increasingly, however, more fodder crops were grown, showing a greater emphasis on cattle. Thus in March 1747 Francis Best of Pershore had £110 worth of hay, 30 acres of clover and 53 acres of peas to support a herd of 26 cows and 12 calves, compared with only 45 acres of grain.

As previously, the Vale of Evesham was renowned for its fertility. In 1725 Daniel Defoe wrote 'The product of the soil is very plentiful in corn ... almost to a miracle in the Vale of Evesham ... the country is famous for the good cheese and butter, for fruits, especially pears, which grow in every hedge ...'. Vegetables were another local product, with labourers around Evesham noted for their gardening skills, and with a land-owning system which favoured the kind of small holding best suited to horticulture. Such traditions attracted other specialists, among them Francis Bernardi, a former Genoese ambassador, who moved to Evesham after the Restoration, and had 'the greatest fame of all gentlemen ... for fine gardens'.

81 Needles being sharpened by a Redditch labourer

VIII *Upton-on-Severn, looking north-west towards the Malvern Hills. The German-style cupola was added to the church tower in 1769-70*

IX *Booth Hall or The Round House, a late 15th-century timber-framed building in the middle of the Norman market-place at Evesham. It was built as an inn, incorporating small ground-floor shops which had 'colonised' the open market-place. The market place has recently been pedestrianised and enhanced*

X *One of several timber-framed houses in Ombersley. This is a medieval cruck house of four bays, originally with a central open hall. One pair of crucks can be seen on the end gable, though the lower parts are masked with decorated Victorian timber-work.*

XI *The Merchant's House, Bromsgrove, now at the Avoncroft Museum of Buildings. The house was built at the end of the l5th century, using the standard medieval plan of solar wing (left), open living hall (right) and service block (demolished but foundations marked with stones). In the l6th century the house was occupied by the families of Richard Lylley (d.l558), dyer, and his son Reginald (d.l586), dyer and weaver*

XII *St Nicholas's parish church, King's Norton. The l5th-century tower and spire was described by John Leland c.l540 as 'a goodly piramis of stone'. The building to the right, parts of which also date from the l5th century, was originally the priest's house but became the grammar school in the l6th century. The painting is by A. E. Everitt, the l9th-century Birmingham painter*

Especially in the sheltered Teme valley, hops continued to be another speciality. In 1718 the rector of Stanford-on-Teme had 15,000 hop poles, while in 1747 the mixed farm of Richard Witney of Tenbury had hops worth £90. In 1794 it was estimated that 'the number of acres planted with hops this year is 5,998', some 1.2 per cent of the surface area of the county. Several towns had hop markets, the best known being at Worcester, where it was held three days a week under the direction of the Hop Market Guardians. Another product of the county was perry, manufactured from pears, the orchards of Monkland Farm, Newland—between Malvern and Worcester—having an especially high reputation.

Pastoral farming occurred throughout the county. Cobbett, in 1826, described the huge meadows of the Avon valley, where 'nine tenths of the land appears to me to be pasture', and where 'the number of cattle and sheep ... is prodigious'. Usually, however, animal husbandry was mixed with cultivation, as in the south-eastern Cotswold fringe, where farmers grew grain in the valleys and grazed sheep on the interlocking hills.

The greatest changes occurred in the north-east of the county. This was traditionally a pastoral area with rural metal-working, but the expanding industries on the adjacent south Staffordshire coalfield now induced a number of changes. New techniques enabled grain production to be increased, so that in the 1660s 'the markett way' to Stourbridge from Chaddesley Corbett was one of a number of tracks which began to deteriorate under the burden of an increased traffic of grain wagons. Simultaneously livestock numbers increased, the mean size of herds of cattle and flocks of sheep rising by some 50 per cent in the parishes of Belbroughton, Bromsgrove and Chaddesley Corbett during the 17th century. These processes encouraged some farmers in these and neighbouring parishes to abandon metalworking altogether, scyth-making, for example, moving out of Clent into Halesowen.

Manufacturing

The late 17th century saw great developments in the manufacture of iron in the north-west of the county. The Forest of Wyre and other woodlands supplied charcoal; steeply falling streams provided water power for the blast-furnaces, forges and slitting mills; and the River Severn could be used to assemble iron ores from Shropshire, the Forest of Dean and abroad. The industry was controlled by great dynasties, like the Foleys and the Wheelers of Stourbridge, whose works dominated the Stour valley, or the Knights of Bringewood in Herefordshire, who had outposts at Wolverley near Kidderminster.

The use of coal rather than charcoal to smelt iron ore was developed in Shropshire by Abraham Darby in 1709, but it took another 50 years for the process to be perfected. The potential of the South Staffordshire coalfield, which overlapped into north Worcestershire, began to be developed in 1772, when John Wilkinson, 'the iron king', built an ironworks just outside Dudley. By 1794 there were 14 such furnaces on the coalfield, producing more than 13,000 tons of iron a year. The greater abundance of iron boosted the traditional metal-working industries of north Worcestershire, especially the manufacture of nails and needles.

82 Industrial smoke blowing up over historic Dudley, in this engraving reproduced by Nash in 1799

*83 Small factories
and low quality
factories later
developed around the
urban canals, as here
at Lowesmoor Wharf,
Worcester, in
the 1940s*

The 1831 census shows that 2,751 people were employed in nail-making in Worcestershire, most of them in Bromsgrove, Dudley and Northfield. The industry was organised by nail-masters, who supplied rod iron on a weekly basis to nailers working in their own premises. Most of the nailers were poor and lived in small cottages, often with the husband having another part-time job. Needle-manufacture, as in earlier periods, was concentrated in the valley of the River Arrow, with Alcester in Warwickshire and Redditch in Worcestershire as the main centres. The work was hard and dangerous, especially scouring and sharpening the needles, which produced dust that clogged and poisoned lungs.

All over the county, the market towns and larger villages retained traditional industries, especially tanning, corn milling and brewing; but nearly everywhere cloth manufacture, for long the staple industry, fell into rapid decline, unable to compete with more favourably endowed areas like the Gloucestershire Cotswolds and the West Riding of Yorkshire. At Bewdley, however, the traditional craft of cap-making survived to the mid-18th century, while at Kidderminster the age-old weaving skills were diverted into the new boom trade of carpet manufacture.

Recent research for the 1660-1760 period has identified the inventories of 25 Bewdley cappers. Most were valued at less than £100, but Anthony Smith (d.1726), a member of the Corporation, had an estate worth £963 5s. The most informative inventory is that of Henry Wolloxall (d.1683), whose goods were valued at £148 15s. 8d. He had 'coloured, white and medley wool' worth £30 3s. 4d. in the house, while his tools included 'a colouring furnace' and 'a stocking frame', as well as 'blocks and netts and other implements'. His stock of caps had the high value of £102 10s., many of them already being in London, the chief marketing outlet for the industry.

Personal enterprise was responsible for the start of carpet manufacture in Kidderminster, in place of the ailing production of the chequered cloths known as 'Kidderminster stuffs'. The first factory was established in 1735 in Mill Street, near the River Stour, whose waters, it was later claimed, gave 'brilliancy and durableness' to the carpets. A few years later a local manufacturer, John Broom, brought in a Belgian weaver from Brussels, who revealed the secrets of a long established trade, and allowed Kidderminster to compete effectively with the high quality products of Axminster and Wilton. In 1753 Lord Foley, a descendant of the iron-master, injected capital to build 200 new houses and lay out streets, and by 1807 there were 1,000 carpet looms at work.

Industrial espionage was involved in the success of another Worcestershire industry, the manufacture of glass. This had been started by migrants from Lorraine in France, who found the clay near Stourbridge particularly suitable for making the moulds in which the molten glass was set. Their descendant, Joshua Henzey, formed a partnership in the 1660s with the versatile Foley family, but other glass-masters emerged, such as Thomas Rogers, whose great-grandson became high sheriff in 1750. At first Stourbridge was known for making coloured window glass, but technical innovations made after 1780 led to a high reputation in cut and crystal glass. Many of these were pirated by a local man, George Ensall, who penetrated German glass houses disguised as a minstrel.

Personal enterprise was also shown in the establishment of the manufacture of fine bone china and porcelain at Worcester. This was introduced by Dr. John Wall,

*84 The Worcester
Porcelain Manufactory
in 1752, fronting on
to the River Severn.
Clay from Cornwall
and other materials
were brought up river*

who leased premises overlooking the Severn in 1751. The river was used to import china clay from Cornwall, but apart from good communications there were no other locational advantages. A company was established which was one of the first to introduce transfer-printing, which was much cheaper than hand-painting and so brought decorated wares to a wider market. Thomas Flight, previously the firm's London agent, acquired the business in 1783, and earned the title Worcester Royal Porcelain Company by persuading George III to make a visit in 1788.

Another adjustment to the loss of Worcester's cloth-making industry was the expansion of glove manufacture, which had been present in the city since the Middle Ages, but catering primarily for local need. The industry thrived during the Napoleonic wars, when continental imports were restricted. Most of the gloves were sold wholesale to London merchants or exported to the colonies or the United States, but the removal of prohibition on the import of cheaper European gloves in 1826 caused sudden decline and brought great hardship to the city. The industry was organised by more than a hundred 'glover masters'. They employed glove cutters in their small factories, but the leather was sent out to women and children outworkers, who stitched the gloves in their own homes. Some of the leading glove-masters, such as John Dent (d.1811) or George Allen (d.1824) had manufactories in Sidbury, but the outworkers were spread all over the city, concentrated especially in the parishes of St Martin's and St Peter's.

Transport by water and land

The River Severn remained the major artery of trade. In 1724 Daniel Defoe claimed that the Severn was navigable 'by large barges' as far as Welshpool, though a later account qualified this by adding 'after a fashion' for the stretch above Bewdley. It has been shown that 'there was more traffic on the Severn at the end of the 17th century than on any other river in Europe', except for a section of the Meuse in the Low Countries. The Avon was also navigable to above Evesham.

George Perry, writing in *The Gentleman's Magazine* in 1758, described vessels 'of two sorts'. The smaller, carrying 20 to 40 tons, were called barges or frigates, and had one mast; the larger, carrying 40 to 80 tons, were called trows, and had two or three masts. These vessels could sail downstream, with the current in their favour, but they had to be towed upstream by horses or by gangs of men, as noted by Celia Fiennes in 1698, when she observed at Worcester 'many Barges that were tow'd up by the strength of men 6 or 8 at a time'. In the late 17th and early 18th centuries more vessels were based at Worcester, Bewdley, Upton-on-Severn and other Worcestershire river ports than in any other county, but the later development of the Broseley/Coalbrookdale industrial area saw more craft further up the river. Thus in 1758, out of 376 vessels only 93 had home ports in Worcestershire, compared with 245 in Shropshire.

Port books and other records testify to the great volume and diversity of the cargoes carried on the Severn. Those coming upstream included iron ore from the Forest of Dean and imported haematite from Spain and Sweden, needed for the furnaces of the Stour valley and Coalbrookdale; a range of grocery, such as fruit, spices, and tobacco; Irish and Spanish wool for making textiles; and quantities of 'train oil', fish oil used for fuelling lamps and for curreying leather. Goods going

85 One of the trows which carried a variety of cargoes up and down the River Severn. The trows were about 60 ft. long and some 18 ft. wide

the other way included pig iron, rod iron and iron wares as diverse as locks, frying pans and buckets; different kinds of glass from the Stourbridge area; pot clay from Amblecote, sent to London and elsewhere for making earthenware; a range of textiles such as the chequered cloths called Kidderminster stuff and the cottons known as Manchester ware; salt from Droitwich and Cheshire; and a number of specialised Worcestershire products such as the 7,500 scythe-stones sent down river in 1701.

Especially for bulky goods, water transport was so superior to that on land at this time that there were frequent attempts to improve navigation, and to build canals. The ascendancy of Birmingham and the adjoining Black Country towns made it particularly desirable to build canals up to the Birmingham plateau, though this would entail staircases of locks. Encouraged by the completion of the Bridgewater canal in Lancashire, a group of investors secured an Act of Parliament in 1766 to build the Staffordshire and Worcestershire canal from the Severn to south Staffordshire, utilising the Stour valley as a route and employing 'the half-illiterate genius' James Brindley as engineer. This canal was opened in 1770, and two years later was joined by the Birmingham canal, with great public rejoicing as the first coal barge arrived at the new Gas Street basin. A smaller canal linking Droitwich to the Severn was opened in 1771, but the boldest undertaking was the Birmingham to Worcester canal. After a petition with 6,058 signatures had been

86 *Part of the river port of Bewdley in the late 18th century, after much of its trade had been lost to Stourport. It shows Bewdley Old Bridge, prior to its destruction by floods in 1795. This had replaced an earlier bridge in 1483. The Bridge Gate House, which accommodated a toll-gatherer and a prison, can be clearly seen*

submitted, an Act of Parliament was secured in 1791, but the canal, starting from Birmingham, did not reach Worcester until 1815. The steepest gradient was surmounted by the Tardebigge flight of 30 locks, leading up to the Tardebigge tunnel.

Nearly all passengers and much freight traffic still went by roads, which were also improved during this period. Ogilby's *Road Atlas* of 1676 showed a number of routes crossing the county, most of them converging on Worcester. There were of course other important routes not included by Ogilby, such as that across the Severn at Bewdley. During the 18th century, however, as towns in the north of the county grew in importance, a new network asserted itself, with a number of turnpike roads converging on Birmingham. The first was the Bromsgrove turnpike in 1726, which eventually reached to Worcester, followed by the Hagley turnpike of 1753 and the Dudley turnpike of 1760. Improved road surfaces here and elsewhere enabled new services to be started, reaching sometimes to the remoter parts of the county, as in 1758, when the postal service from London was extended to Great Malvern, then only a small village, but poised to benefit from this 'first regular link with the outside world'.

87 *One of the staircase of locks near Tardebigge, as the Worcester to Birmingham canals climbs up on to the Birmingham plateau*

The countryside and its great houses

The 18th century saw the apogee of the English 'great house'; and the 18th-century country houses of Worcestershire have been described as 'a large chapter'. They stood in the centre of vast parks, many of which still survive, such as that of Hagley Hall, now dissected by the A456 from Kidderminster to Birmingham. They were

*88 Ham Court,
Upton-on-Severn,
built for the Martins
in 1772 by
Anthony Keck.
It was demolished
in 1925*

sustained by the rents of tenant farmers and by other sources of income often far from their own gates, as at Great Witley, bought and rebuilt by the Foleys from the profits of their ironworks. Their owners were prominent in local affairs, serving as justices of the peace and as colonels of the local militia or county regiments. Many of them served as members of parliament and a few found the energy for a political career, for example Thomas Winnington of Stanford-on-Teme, who was Paymaster General during the 1745 Jacobite rebellion. Many left behind them ostentatious memorials, as at Croome d'Abitot, where the church has the tombs of generations of the Earls of Coventry, including that of the fourth earl (d.1687) carved by Grinling Gibbons, the leading sculptor of the day.

Some great families made very few alterations to earlier houses, as at Rous Lench Court in the far east of the county. A 16th- and early 17th-century timber-framed house was left unaltered, by both the Rouses and then by the Rouse Boughtons who succeeded them in 1721, though there was a substantial rebuilding about 1840. In other cases, small, up-to-date additions were made, such as the porch at Hartlebury Castle, or there were internal alterations, as at Westwood, where the Packingtons inserted a new grand staircase and gave the great chamber a magnificent new plaster ceiling, rich with wreaths of fruit and foliage. Where funds permitted, however, it was fashionable to rebuild, and some 40 great houses were erected in Worcestershire during the period of this chapter.

Architecturally, Worcestershire was a conservative county. Details such as Dutch gables, shaped gables with a pediment on top, did not arrive until the 1670s, 40 years after they were introduced in London. By the end of the 17th century, however, the kind of symmetrical plan and façade associated with Christopher Wren and his followers, with well proportioned detailing and restrained classical ornament, was established in the county. Medium-sized houses of this kind, popularly described as 'Georgian', were erected all over the county during the next century. Examples include Middle Hall, Broadway, built with five bays about 1725 and later the home of Sir Thomas Phillips, a noted bibliophile; Ham Court (now demolished), Upton-on-Severn, built in 1772 for the Martins of Martins Bank; and Craycombe House, Fladbury, built in 1791 for George Perrott of the East India Company, but later the home of Francis Brett Young, the Worcestershire novelist.

Especially in the early years the taste was classical. This is most apparent at Hewell Grange, Tardebigge, the former home of the Earls of Plymouth, for behind a Victorian refronting is a huge two-storey hall, dating from about 1700, where 'the visitor is transported suddenly and without warning to Italy'. Later in the century, when several parks were landscaped by 'Capability' Brown and Humphry Repton, many classical monuments were erected, including the imitation Temple of Theseus at Hagley in 1758. This is the first copy of a Greek Doric-style temple anywhere in Europe, and reflects the interest of English landowners in the world of antiquity, as witnessed on the grand tour which normally completed their education. The grounds at Hagley also contain a ruined castle, designed as such by Sanderson Miller, an architect with an interest in the Middle Ages. Their work led to the Gothic Revival, of which an early Worcestershire example was Lea Castle (now demolished) at Cookley, north of Kidderminster, a battlemented, asymmetrical building built for the Knights, close to their iron-works at Wolverley.

Architecturally, two of the finest houses of this period are Hanbury Hall, south of Bromsgrove, and Croome Court, Croome d'Abitot, between Malvern and Pershore. Hanbury Hall, with its 'beautifully balanced façade of soft red brick', has been eulogised as 'the very essence of the English country house'. It was completed in 1701 for Thomas Vernon (d.1721), a celebrated lawyer, whose family had bought the manor in 1631. The 11-bay façade contains two projecting wings of three bays each, and a central pedimented block, flanked by giant columns on pedestals, and crowned by a cupola. The glory of the house is the great staircase, rising from the central hall and adorned by large figure scenes, painted by Sir James Thornhill, the leading English mural painter of his day. Croome Court, built some 50 years later in golden Bath stone, is also of 11 bays, but in the correct, severely classical style known as Palladian which was then in vogue. It has a pedimented portico over the central three bays, and square towers at the sides. One of the finest rooms is the long gallery, with its 'sumptuous chimneypiece', which was designed by Robert Adam, the doyen of internal decorators from 1760.

The plans of these and other houses were designed for entertaining in the grand manner, as well as for living and administration. This is well illustrated at Hagley Hall, built at the same time as Croome Court. It has the usual 18th-century axis of entrance hall in front, with saloon behind, but these are part of a planned socialising circuit on the eastern side of the house, which included drawing room, gallery and dining room. These rooms could accommodate receptions and assemblies of various kinds, as well as the occasional grand county ball.

The towns

At the beginning of this period all Worcestershire towns were relatively small. A census of churchgoers made in 1676, on the order of Archbishop Compton, suggests that Worcester, though ranked the 12th largest town in England in 1662, had a population of less than 5,000 people. A second tier of towns included Dudley, Bewdley, Bromsgrove and Kidderminster, all with more than 2,000 residents, but Droitwich, Evesham, Halesowen, Pershore, Stourbridge and Tenbury each had less than 1,500 inhabitants. Smaller still were towns such as Alvechurch, Broadway and Upton-on-Severn, with probably less than 500 people.

By 1801, the year of the first government census, all these towns had grown in size by at least 50 per cent, and in many cases by much more. The most remarkable increase was at Halesowen, which leapt to 5,867 in 1801, and to 9,765 in 1831. In 1801 the largest town in the county was Dudley, with a population of 19,107, but by 1831 Worcester, which nearly doubled in size between 1801 and 1831, shared first place, both having some 23,000 residents. The market towns of the south also grew rapidly, with Evesham and Pershore each having some 4,000 people in 1831, while at Great Malvern, a small village in 1676, the development of a fashionable spa increased the population from 951 in 1801 to 2,140 in 1831.

Weekly markets and fairs several times a year remained a basic function of nearly all Worcestershire towns. Evesham, for example, set in the most agriculturally productive part of the county, had a weekly Monday market and three yearly fairs. The latter, according to Nash, were famous 'for the sale of strong black horses'.

89 *The Temple of Theseus in the grounds of Hagley Hall. It was designed by James 'Athenian' Stuart in 1758*

The flavour of the weekly market is caught by Ben Boucher, a local collier-poet, in his 'Lines on Dudley Market 1827':

'At Dudley market now I tell,
Most kind of articles they sell;
The women take the greatest care
To buy up crocks and earthenware,
Milkpans and colliers' tots,
Coloured cups and chamber pots.
At the top of the Shambles Sally stands,
She holds the basket in her hands:
'Now my good people don't be lacking
Here you may buy the best of blacking';
In Stoney Street there stands the swine,
Both right and left all in a line;
They sell these pigs so much per score,
So on that street I'll say no more'.

To accommodate the increasing population, many new dwellings were erected within the long established built-up areas of towns. In-filling and back building along medieval burgage plots were commonplace, as is clear from a study of large-scale Ordnance Survey maps at Bewdley, Evesham, Pershore and elsewhere. Housing became particularly dense at Worcester, as is illustrated by recent tenurial reconstructions of Friar Street and Blackfriars. The plot now occupied by 17, 19, 21, 23 and 25 Friar Street, for example, on the corner with Union Street, had contained just three houses in the 16th century, built by Robert Voyle who acquired the site from the dissolved Franciscan friary. By 1678 there were rows of three or four cottages behind 17 and 25, both probably inns, while the central block, now 19-23, was rebuilt in 1739 with cottages at the rear. The city plan book of 1784 shows there were then 11 dwellings on the site, but in the 19th

90 A view of Dudley from the east c.1775, when it was beginning a rapid transformation from a small market town into a major industrial centre

1.	St John's	8.	All Saint's Church	15.	The Bifhop's Palace	21.	The Priory-moat
2.	Pitchcroft	9.	St Nicholas' Church	16.	The Guild-hall	22.	King Edgar's Tower
3.	Severn-bridge	10.	St Andrew's Church	17.	St Helen's Church	23.	The County Gaol
4.	St Clement's Church	11.	St Swithin's Church	18.	St Mary's Cathedral	24.	The Caftle-hill
5.	City water-works	12.	St Martin's Church	19.	The College-hall	25.	St Peter's Church
6.	The Key	13.	St Alban's Church	20.	The Old Priory Infirmary	26.	Perry-wood
7.	Berkley's Hofpital	14.	The Porcelain Manufactory				

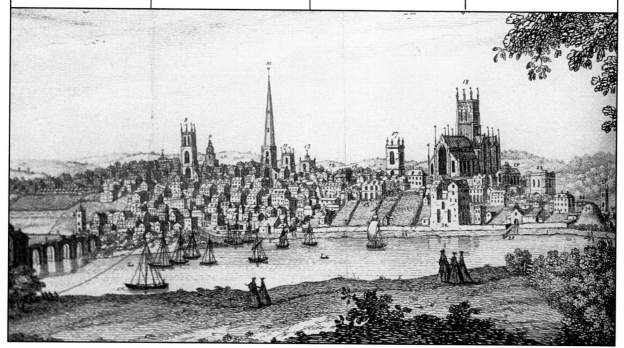

century this number had risen to about 18 houses and a number of privies and other outbuildings, arranged round long, narrow yards known as Courts three and four.

In other towns new streets had to be laid out to accommodate the extra houses. In Kidderminster, where carpet manufacture was burgeoning, the triangle between Hall Street/Barn Street, Black Star Street and Church Street was divided into four by Orchard Street and Paddock Street. The intended developments were marked on an *Exact Plan of Kidderminster*, published by John Doharty in 1753, 'in which the New Streets are inserted as intended to be Built'. Here and in some of the older streets, such as Mill Street, there was soon gross overcrowding, and in 1781 Nash reported that 'the houses and shops not being sufficiently airy and clean, fevers for the most part take a putrid turn'.

Whilst some parts of 18th-century towns suffered high densities and insanitary conditions, there was also an urge by gentry, professional and successful business classes to build new, fashionable houses in the elegant styles of the day, with brick as the prime building material. One of the first was Dresden House in Evesham, a five-bay house built in 1692, with an open pediment over the central entrance. A three-storey summer-house was added about 1750. Other impressive houses still standing include Finch House in

91 *An engraving of Worcester seen from the south-west in 1764. In addition to the cathedral, nine medieval churches are visible, as well as the bridge across the Severn built in 1313, the priory infirmary (in front of the cathedral) and the Norman castle motte (far right)*

92 *Dresden House, Evesham, which has a date of 1692 on its rainwater head*

93 *A five-bay house in Church Street, Broadway, which was built about 1700. There are impressive gate piers.*

Dudley, built for a rich ironmonger in 1707, and Perrott House, Pershore, built about 1760 for Judge Perrott, a Baron of the Exchequer. The latter has a number of Venetian windows, a favourite Worcestershire motif, and delicate interior stucco work. Many developers built terraces, for example at Bridge Street, Worcester, when the building of a new bridge, completed in 1780, gave opportunity for land acquisition. The project was described by Nash, who wrote: 'On the city side is intended an entire new street of forty feet width, letting in a beautiful view of Malvern hills ...'. Attempts to improve towns in this way were characteristic of the period after 1720. Parliament passed a number of 'private' Improvement Acts allowing individuals, usually called commissioners, to fund and bring in specified services and alterations, the first for Worcestershire being the paving and widening of streets in Droitwich in 1755. There were three such Acts for Worcester, in 1770, 1771 and 1780, which provided for the new bridge, an improved public water supply and the first street lights. There were similar schemes at Kidderminster (1760 and 1822), Dudley (1791), Stourbridge (1791) and Evesham, the latter involving the sale of land, as well as a new bridge, street cleaning and paving, and the organisation of a public order watch.

94 *Perrott House, Pershore, built about 1760, with canted bays and Venetian windows*

95 *Waterside House, Upton-on-Severn, built in the early 18th century*

96 *The central bays of the exterior of Worcester Guildhall, completed in 1724*

Corporations, voluntary bodies and public subscription provided other facilities in this 'Age of Improvement'. These included a second new bridge over the Severn, that was built for the Bridge Wardens at Bewdley by Thomas Telford in 1795-98; a new building in 1767 in Castle Street, Worcester, for the county's first medical hospital, the Royal Infirmary, which had been founded in 1745; and a number of town halls, guildhalls and assembly rooms. Most town halls were modest, for example that built in the Grecian style at Upton-on-Severn in 1832, but the new Guildhall at Worcester, designed by local architect Thomas White and finished in 1723, is 'as splendid as any 18th century Town Hall in England'. There were a number of rooms, including two court rooms, and on the upper floor a long dual purpose room, used both as a council chamber and as the assembly room. In 1764 the building was praised for having 'every accommodation for a genteel reception of the nobility and the gentry ...'.

Two distinctive towns were Stourport and Great Malvern. Stourport is almost unique as a canal town, which came into existence where the new Staffordshire and Worcester canal joined the Severn in 1770. A complex of Georgian buildings around the basins includes the *Tontine Inn*, opened in 1788, and an early 19th-century warehouse adorned with a cupola. Great Malvern developed as a village spa in the 17th century, the first known water cure patient being Mary Smith, a lame woman from Clains, who in 1672 'set out to goe to Malverne Well in hope of some benefitt by that water'. The water cure was publicised in 1757 by Dr. Wall, a native of Powick who became one of the original physicians at Worcester Infirmary. He claimed that the efficacy of the waters came from their purity due to there being very low mineral content, causing a wag to remark that: 'The Malvern water, says Dr. John Wall Is famed for containing just nothing at all'.

Hotels followed in due course, and the completion of the pump room and baths in 1823 established the growing town as a fashionable spa, which in 1830 had the accolade of a visit from the Princess Victoria.

Goods and chattels: a case study

The availability of probate inventories for the first century of this period provides a number of glimpses into the life styles of a wide range of Worcestershire people, even though there is some bias towards the richer sections of the community. Of the thousands of these documents lying in the County Record Office and the Public Record Office in London, this section draws on a sample of 565 inventories from Bewdley, Ribbesford and Wribbenhall (part of Kidderminster parish) for the 1660-1760 period.

The inventories, which assess moveable goods but not property, show a wide range of estate values. 433 inventories, over three quarters of the total, had values of less than £100, and of these 230, two-fifths of the total, had less than £20. At the other extreme were a number of very rich grocers and mercers, who profited from their good trading position to the extent that nine of them had estates of over £1,000, with four over £2,000.

The inventories of a number of tradesmen known to have lived around Bewdley market-place illustrate the differing life styles of near neighbours in the years after the Restoration. Samuel Clare (d.1674), who lived up an alley somewhere near the present *Wheatsheaf Inn* on the south side of Load Street, was assessed at only £5 11s., and was rated a pauper by the 1664 Hearth Tax assessors. He had basic furniture and three flock beds, but only three pairs of sheets and just four pewter dishes. William Holmes (d.1662), dyer, who lived at 44 Load Street, was assessed at £19 13s. 00d. Shears and other equipment in his shop, including 'Brasile and other colouring stuff', accounted for 17s. of this amount. He, his wife and his children lived in a two-room house, with a heated hall and an unheated chamber or bedroom. He had five beds and five mattresses, with 14 pairs of sheets, all in the chamber, and a number of chests and coffers for storage. The hall had tables, chairs and wainscoting, an iron grate and utensils around the hearth, and a certain amount of brass and pewter ware, including one chamber pot. A much richer man was William Clare (d.1668), a baker and also landlord of the *George Inn*, a little nearer towards the bridge. One of The Twelve, William Clare, had goods worth £233 3s. 2d., and was assessed for five hearths in 1664, though this later rose to eight, no doubt as the inn was extended. As well as a number of feather beds, equipped with 'curtains and vallences', he had such luxuries as a close stool, 18 cushions, a livery table and £3 10s.-worth of silver-ware.

Much richer again was Thomas Wootton (d.1667), grocer, who had a 12-room house and a shop on the other side of the street, on part of what is now the Town Hall site. Wootton, a member of The Twelve who was bailiff in the eventful year of 1660, was assessed at the remarkable total of £6,227 8s. 6d., though nearly half of this consisted of debts from customers scattered throughout the west Midlands, from Coventry in the east to Welshpool in central Wales in the west. Wootton's luxury items included silver plate worth £94 10s. and gold pieces worth £7 17s. 4d., a number of pictures in the hall and parlour, two coats of arms, a looking-glass and one parrot, the last a very rare item indeed!

For the more affluent, the century after the Restoration saw a notable rise in living standards. One measure is the number of pairs of sheets per bedstead, which increased at Bewdley from 2.01 for the period 1660-1709 to 3.50 for the period 1710-59. The proportion of inventories recording at least one looking-glass increases from 11.6 per cent for the 1660-79 period, to 24 per cent for 1740-59. Earthenware, a welcome change from the ubiquitous pewter, occurs in only 3.3 per cent of inventories from 1669-1679, but this increases to 15.4 per cent for 1740-59, including eight references to Delph ware, for example the 'nine Delph plates' in the home of John Gowan (d.1742), capper. For the first 60 years of the period, clocks and watches are extremely rare, occurring in only 4.8 per cent of inventories, mostly those of gentry, professional men or leading tradesmen. After 1720, however, clocks and cases become much more common, and are found in homes as socially diverse as those of Thomas Pagett (d.1726), wheelwright, Samuel Price (d.1735), waterman and John Warrall (d.1750), nailer.

Though unrecorded by probate inventories in large numbers, the comfort of daily life continued to improve, especially for the affluent middle class. In 1803 the house of Robert Pardoe, lawyer, in Park Lane, Bewdley, had 12 main rooms, with a number of cellars, service rooms and attics, containing articles valued at £901 6s. 2d. Items of interest include 'a weather glass' made in London, a number of pictures including *Horse and Men* by Stubbs, a quantity of mahogany furniture,

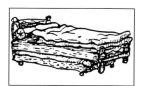

97 A 17th-century bedstead, with a mattress (bed) and coverings above, and a trundle bed below. The latter was pushed under the bedstead when not in use

utensils for making and serving tea and a considerable quantity of china. The 'two dozen of Doyleys' in the dining room sideboard and 'the twelve Cups and saucers with Gold Edge with a small blue and yellow flower' are among several items which hint at the style of social life in the age of Jane Austen, even in a declining river port such as Bewdley.

At the other end of the High Street, however, in the congested back alleys and courts of Welch Gate, life was very different. A few years previously Dr. Prattinton, a local antiquarian, had attempted to carry out a census 'above the Gate', but had to make an estimate for this part of the town because, he recorded, 'the Poor were so offended and so clamorous, It was prudent to desist'.

The Poor

Regulation of the poor and provision for their relief were continuing concerns during this period. Bequests to the poor remained common, as at Bromsgrove, where in 1676 Simon Hill, yeoman, left '20s. to be divided between eight poor', while in 1688 Mary Smith, widow, gave £5 for the poor 'to be given door to door'. Others left larger sums for investment, for example in the parish of Inkberrow, where there were five bequests of land or rent charges between 1672 and 1786. The foundation of almshouses continued from time to time, as those at Rock, erected in 1724 by the Rev. J. Walls, D. D., 'for the support and maintenance of six distressed widows'. Endowments of this kind supplemented poor relief, a rate levied on all who could afford to pay. At Great Malvern this was £156 17s. 8d. in 1778, but had risen to £267 9s. 0½d. in 1785, due to a series of poor harvests.

The money collected was used in a variety of ways. Part it of went on out-relief, payments to the poor in their own homes. In the large parish of Belbroughton, for example, which had a population of 1,476 in 1831, there was an average of 68 weekly payments in that year, with sums ranging from 6s. to 1s. Sometimes the gifts were made in kind, as in the same parish in 1828, when there were 22 instances of grants of clothing, materials or bedding. There were some occasional payments for a particular purpose, as in Great Malvern in 1778, when 5s. 5d. was paid for 'thatching ye widow Tompkins house'.

The most drastic solution to the problems posed by the poor was to send them to a workhouse. Such an institution was established in Worcester in 1703, due to a recent increase in the number of poor people. Guardians were appointed to administer the workhouse and to contract with other parishes for receiving and putting the poor to work. They were to compel 'beggars and idle people' to work in the workhouse, while poor children found begging were to be kept at work until 15 years old, when they were to be bound apprentice for seven years.

Poor people could only claim parish relief if they had settlement, a status often hotly contested by the parish. A person could only remain in a new parish if he had a settlement certificate to show that his former parish would support him should he become chargeable on the poor rate. Removal orders were served to those with no right of settlement, as at Hanley Castle, where at least 111 people were forcibly removed from the parish between 1717 and 1835, while in the same period 117 were returned to Hanley. Pregnant single women were often involved, like the one escorted back to Hanley Castle from Bristol in 1830, after an affair with a married shoemaker.

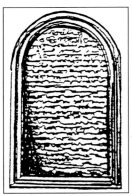

98 The charity board in Wolverley church which records a gift made in 1823 by John Smith Esq. of Blakeshall House, to fund a weekly Sunday evening sermon, with the balance of '8s. 8d. to go to the poor.'

Conformists and Nonconformists

Religious contention and persecution continued during the early decades of this period. Between 1662 and 1665, the new government of Charles II introduced a number of acts, known as the Clarendon Code. This forced clergy to conform to the prayer-book, made church attendance compulsory, forbade other meetings for worship and banned dissenting ministers from teaching and from living within five miles of a town. There were more than 95 inductions to Worcestershire livings at this time, many of them replacing clergy such as Richard Moore from Alvechurch and Thomas Franks from Naunton Beauchamp. The most notorious displacement was that of Richard Baxter, the puritanical divine, who had to give way at Kidderminster to the former vicar, George Dance.

99 *Friends' Meeting House at Scott's Road, Stourbridge, built in 1688. It contains a single room with a gallery*

In spite of the Clarendon Code, nonconformity took root in many parts of the county. The Declaration of 1672 recognised this by suspending penal laws and allowing a number of buildings to be licensed for worship. The Presbyterians were strongest in the north of the county, but the Independents/Congregationalists were scattered in the centre and south-east. By 1693 the number of nonconformists in Worcestershire was given as 1,325, 3.3 per cent of all adult worshippers, but that is probably an under-estimate. The oldest standing chapel is the Presbyterian meeting house in Lower High Street, Stourbridge, built in 1698, two years after the minister, George Flower, came to the area as chaplain to Philip Foley, a local iron-master. A treasured relic is the pulpit used by Richard Baxter, now at the New Meeting House, Kidderminster.

Toleration for Quakers, Anabaptists and Roman Catholics was given less readily. For the Quakers persecution was always a threat, as in 1673, when the national leader, George Fox, visited a meeting in Tredington, only to be arrested and imprisoned. Again, the earliest surviving meeting house is that at Stourbridge, in Scott's Road, on a site acquired in 1688. Like the slightly later meeting house at Bewdley, it is a single room with a gallery. The Anabaptists were strongest in the east, where they appealed mainly to poorer people, two congregations at Kington being described in 1669 as each having 'about thirty mean persons'. In 1693, the number of Papists reported in the county was 727, which was 1.8 per cent of all adults, rather more than half the number of nonconformists. This group included a number of landowners and was also numerous in Worcester, where James II, visiting the city in 1687, scandalised the mayor by attending Mass at a Roman Catholic chapel, built in 1685 when the new reign began a short period of toleration. This ended with the Toleration Act of 1689, after the accession of William and Mary, causing such chapels to be destroyed, and Roman Catholics remained without full civil and political rights until the Emancipation Bill of 1829.

For the Church of England, the 18th century is often represented as an arid period, when a quiet exercise of faith was widely practised, though 'enthusiasm' was suspect. Support for this view comes from the biographies of some of the Bishops of Worcester. John Hough (1717-43), for example, is regarded as 'making no history', apart from 'numerous instances of kindness and liberality'; while Brownlow North (d.1781) is remembered primarily as the founder of the Three Choirs Festival, initially as a charity for poor clergy. There was enough vitality, however, to rebuild several parish churches, including four in Worcester between 1730 and 1770, and a number of others in the towns and villages. The latter, all

simple rectangles with round-arched windows and west towers, include those at Stourbridge (1728-36), Smethwick (1728), Bewdley (1745-48) and Upton-on-Severn (1756-57). The most remarkable is the church at Great Witley (1735), built by Thomas Foley IV (d.1766), the great-grandson of Thomas Foley I (d.1677), who had bought the estate from the profits of his iron-making. The exterior is restrained, but the inside is 'the most Italian ecclesiastic space ... in England', due to ceiling paintings by the Venetian, Antonio Belluci, stained glass and other fittings, which were bought in by Foley from a Middlesex house of the Duke of Chandos, built in 1719, but due for demolition in 1747. The church also contains the massive memorial to Thomas Foley III (d.1732), fashioned by the sculptor Michael Rysbrack and claimed to be 'the tallest funerary monument in the country'. Thomas Foley III had been created Baron Foley of Kidderminster and was, the epitaph informs us, 'a man excellently endowed with domestic and public virtues', though his elevation to the peerage was also due to being a brother-in-law of Robert Harley, chief minister to Queen Anne.

New energies came to the Church of England from a number of directions, beginning with Wesleyanism, for the growth of which 1739 was a crucial year, with John Wesley's mission to Bristol. Wesley himself is not recorded as visiting Worcestershire until 1761, when he preached to 'a poor scattered society at Evesham', but during later journeys he found local churches thriving, with 'the flame still increasing' in the late 1770s. A chapel of 1772 in New Street, Worcester, survives from these formative years, though now divided, with shops on the ground floor. An early chapel still in use is that in High Street, Stourport, where a Methodist society was formed in 1781, within a few years of the opening

XIII *Hanbury Hall, completed in 1701 for Thomas Vernon, a successful barrister. The composed, well proportioned front elevation is the quintessence of the Wren style and is often praised for its 'Englishness'*

XIV *Hagley Hall, built in the Palladian tradition for Lord Lyttelton in the late 1750s. Distinctive features include the four corner towers and the large open staircase of two arms to the raised entrance*

XV *Harvington Hall, the brick manor house of the Packingtons, a leading Roman Catholic family. The main range is on the left, with the windows of the Great Chamber (solar) block in the middle of the picture*

XVI *The view west from Trimpley, in the parish of Kidderminster, looking across the Severn Valley and Wyre Forest towards the Clee Hills of south east Shropshire*

of the canal. Another breakaway movement from Anglicanism was that of the Evangelicals, who originally worked within the church, but left in 1782, when the Countess of Huntingdon set up her own 'Connexion'. This movement became well established in Worcestershire, with early chapels surviving at Cradley (1789) and Evesham (1789), though the most elaborate is that at Birdport, Worcester (1804-05).

Politics and Reform

After its centre-stage role during the Civil War and Commonwealth, Worcestershire enjoyed a relatively quiet political history during the late 17th and 18th centuries. A number of clergymen, including the Bishop and the Dean of Worcester, were unwilling to take the oath of allegiance to William and Mary in 1688, but with these exceptions the county soon settled down to the new system. In 1745, there was a certain amount of sympathy among the gentry towards the Jacobite rising, but there were no disturbances of any kind.

By the 18th century the two party system of Torys and Whigs was well established, with the influential gentry class split between them. For the two county seats, each party held one each from 1715 to 1747, 1761 to 1774 and 1806 to 1832, but the Tories had both seats from 1747 to 1761, and the Whigs had their turn from 1774 to 1784 and from 1831. It was a similar situation in the boroughs, where the numbers of eligible electors varied considerably, with only 38 burgesses voting in Droitwich in 1747, compared with 555 at Evesham in 1818. Corruption and bribery were often rife, as at Evesham in 1830, where both seats, one taken by a Tory, the other by a Whig, were declared void on petition. Election costs were often very heavy, but candidates were prepared to pay highly for a seat in Parliament and for the power and prestige which went with it.

Even had all elections been fairly contested, the system of parliamentary representation was patently unjust, in Worcestershire as elsewhere. In 1831, the boroughs of Droitwich and Worcester each had two members of parliament, though the former had a population of 2,487, and the latter some 23,000. Worst of all, Dudley, with a population equal to that of Worcester, had no representatives at all. Discontent with this and other inequalities had been widespread in the 1780s and was one of the factors behind the so-called Priestley Riots in Birmingham in 1791, which affected Worcestershire when Moseley Hall and other buildings in King's Norton were burnt down.

Political feeling subsided during the Napoleonic wars, but after 1815 the old agitations were renewed. Feeling was particularly strong in the industrial towns of the north, following the lead given in Birmingham by Thomas Attwood and the other instigators of the Political Unions, but eventually there was support for reform from all over Worcestershire. In 1831 the Whigs, who favoured reform, won both county seats and also controlled most of the seven borough seats. There was jubilation therefore on 18 May 1832 when the second edition of the *Birmingham Journal* announced that 'The cause is at last triumphant ... Lord Grey is recalled to office and the Reform Bill will be immediately passed ...'.

101 *After the parish church at Upton-on-Severn had been largely rebuilt in 1756-57, this un-English cupola was added to the medieval tower in 1769-70. It was designed by Anthony Keck*

Chapter 9

Victorian Worcestershire and the years before and after, 1832-1914

102 *The entrance to the walled enclosure erected at Upton-on-Severn in 1832 to be used as a cemetery for cholera victims*

The Victorian Age—a time of contrasts

The 64-year reign of Queen Victoria dominates this 82-year period, which reaches from the passing of the great Reform Bill in 1832 to the outbreak of the First World War in 1914. After the Chartist riots and the fierce political debates on the Corn Laws in the 1840s, the middle years of the period, beginning with the Great Exhibition of 1851, were later seen as a golden age of British political ascendancy and economic prosperity. In the 1870s, however, a series of bad harvests and other reverses caused great difficulties in agriculture, which were acutely felt in Worcestershire where the yield of the soil made such a major contribution to that prosperity. By the end of the century it became apparent that the lead Britain had once enjoyed over other industrial nations was being reduced, and the metal-working region of north-east Worcestershire was one area where fundamental weaknesses were readily exposed. The pomp and circumstance of the Queen's Diamond Jubilee in 1897, celebrated with great joy in almost every Worcestershire town and village, masked real economic problems, and the period up to the débâcle of 1914 is usually seen as a swansong of the rampant Victorian values.

The carpet manufacturers of Kidderminster manifest the spirit of enterprise and self-help which successful Victorians prized highly, but also testify to the miseries of those who were less successful. Some of them had risen from the ranks, as reported in a popular rhyme: 'Some of our masters then you'll see Were weavers then, as well as we ...'.

When they could afford to do so, factory owners signalled their success by moving outside Kidderminster, as did Henry Talbot when he bought the Upper Minton Estate near Stourport in 1834 for £12,000. They justified the move by saying that in Kidderminster 'the very air is tainted with the odour of dyed worsteds'. When Henry Britton, who owned 67 looms and employed 133 workers, became mayor of that ancient Borough in 1839, he attributed his success partly 'to God's blessing' but also 'to my own exertions'. He omitted to mention that 57 of his employees were children and that many of his weavers and dyers lived in conditions of appalling squalor. In 1841, the houses of the poorer Kidderminster weavers were described as 'dirty, small and ill-ventilated', and in 1845 a committee reported that in places there were 'eight, nine or ten to a room'. Contrasts between rich and poor were equally blatant in the countryside. The journal of Emily Pepys, started in 1844, three years after her father's consecration as Bishop of Worcester, describes an idyllic childhood at Hartlebury Castle with riding in the park, dancing until after midnight and boating on the lake. On occasion she accompanied her mother 'on visits to the poor', which, she wrote, 'she so liked ... if they are clean and do not cry as some do'.

As in most counties, the population rose rapidly, from 220,000 in 1831 to 488,355 in 1901. This was in spite of a high infant mortality rate for much of the period, with epidemics still frequent locally, as at Upton-on-Severn in 1832. Here about 50 people died in a month, most of them living in the narrow alleys and close packed houses near the bank of the Severn. After a few days the tolling of the church bell was stopped by the rector, not only because it depressed the healthy but because it took hope from the sick. Housing conditions were even worse in the rapidly expanding industrial towns, in particular at Dudley, where the Superintending Health Inspector, William Lee, commented in 1851 that 'In no other part of England and Wales is the work of human extermination effected in so short a time as ... in Dudley'.

As well as the contrasts in living standards, Victorian and Edwardian Worcestershire had contrasts of landscape. Though often unaware of the poverty which lurked beneath thatched roofs, poets and other writers justifiably eulogised the rural landscape. This attitude is illustrated by a verse of John Drinkwater's delightful poem 'At Grafton', one of the Bredon Hill villages, written between 1908 and 1914:

> God's beauty over Grafton stole into roof and wall,
> And hallowed every pave'd path and every lowly stall,
> And to a woven wonder conspired with one accord
> The labour of the servant, the labour of the Lord.

This is in stark contrast to the account of the Midland Mining Commissioner, who visited the so-called 'Black Country in south Staffordshire and north Worcestershire', in 1843:

> In traversing much of the country ... the traveller appears never to get out of the interminable village, composed of cottages and ordinary houses. In some directions he may travel for miles and may never be out of sight of numerous two-storeyed houses; so that the area covered by bricks and mortar must be immense. These houses, for the most part, are not arranged in continuous streets but are interspaced with blazing furnaces, heaps of burning coal in process of coking, piles of ironstone calcining, forges, pit-banks and engine chimneys; the country being besides intersected with canals, crossing each other at various levels, and the small remaining patches of the surface soil occupied with irregular fields of grass or corn, intermingled with heaps of the refuse of mines or the slag from the blast furnaces.

Farming

Farming continued to be the major employer, occupying a tenth of the population in 1841, though by 1905 the number of farm workers was declining. In the 1830s and 1840s, whilst controversy about the Corn Laws raged in Parliament and elsewhere, life in the Worcestershire countryside was difficult. The 1850s and 1860s, in contrast, were a golden age, with farmers prospering as they supplied food to the expanding towns. Rents could be met and wages were relatively high. Depression, however, followed in the 1870s. A series of bad harvests culminated

103 *Villagers of both sexes and all ages helped with the hay and corn harvests*

in the disasters of 1879, when late snow and a cold May were followed by a very wet summer. There was some recovery later, but farmers now had to compete with cheap grains flooding in from the developing grasslands of North America and the southern continents.

In the middle years of the century, more than half the farm land of Worcestershire was cultivated, with wheat easily the leading crop. Beans were more important than previously and potatoes were grown extensively in some areas, for example around Kidderminster and Hartlebury. After the traumas of the 1870s, however, cereal production dropped dramatically, but the acreage under permanent grass increased by 40 per cent, as farmers over most of the county specialised in milk and other dairy products for the urban markets.

The Vale of Evesham was an exception. Here, fruit growing and market gardening became more important than ever, especially after 1870, causing the population of parishes like Badsey, Hampton Lovett and Offenham almost to double between 1841 and 1901, a contrast to the trend in most rural areas. The improvement of communications, especially the rail links with Birmingham, was an important cause of this prosperity. In 1906 it was estimated that 2,000 tons of garden produce were dispatched per week during the busy part of the season. Such conditions were ideal for entrepreneurs like James Myatt, who pioneered the growth of strawberries after 1870. Other specialities were asparagus, outdoor rhubarb and early vegetables for salads.

Another crop to expand was hops, which increased by some 50 per cent in Worcestershire between 1874 and 1901, principally in the Teme valley. Here, too, techniques changed rapidly, with wirework replacing poles over large areas. Spraying for the prevention of insect and fungus pests progressed steadily, and in 1890 it was estimated that two-thirds of Worcestershire growers regularly performed this operation. But here also there was foreign competition and in 1908 hundreds of Worcestershire hopgrowers attended a protest meeting in Trafalgar Square about the dumping of foreign hops in England.

104 Stallholders at Evesham street market about 1900, from a painting by local artist John Rock

Markets and Fairs

Much agricultural produce, especially livestock, was sold at fairs, which in many places were now held more often than the statute fairs ordained by ancient charters. A trade directory of 1865 lists 92 such fairs, with Worcester and Bromsgrove having one each month, while smaller places such as Feckenham and Clifton-on-Teme had two a year. Some fairs specialised in a particular product, such as the wool fair at Evesham on 14 August or the five-day horsefair at Stourbridge from 20 to 25 March. At most of these fairs, entertainment was less important than previously, a visitor to the fair on 19 September at Worcester in 1877 complaining that there was 'no glitter of gilded caravans, no painted faces, no pigmies, fat people and skeletons'. In most cases, 'livestock market' was a more meaningful term than 'fair', and after about 1850 they were generally moved to new, purpose-built sites, thus greatly relieving congestion in town centres. At Kidderminster, for example, a ratepayers' meeting was held in 1857 'to consider the advisability of erecting a cattle market to prevent the nuisance caused by animals in the streets'. There were often long delays in acquiring a suitable site, however, and at

Kidderminster it was not until June 1871 that the first stone was laid on a new, two-acre site.

At Evesham, the livestock market had been cleared from the streets by the 1880s, though the fruit and vegetable markets stayed in the High Street outside the *Star Hotel* until the opening of the covered markets. A local resident writing in 1907 recalled the nuisances caused by the street livestock markets:

> On these cobble-stones on fair-days was a motley crowd of men and beasts, for the market was held in the street. Here let my conservative mind own to an improvement! The smell on, say, the annual ram fair, which penetrated the drawing room and haunted our slumbers was —well, I need not dilate upon it. Some dear old ladies of my acquaintance on these Mondays were so upset by the sight of the poor, harassed over-driven animals that they invariably "ordered their fly" early and spent the day out of sight and sound, at the then pretty rural village of Hampton!

105 *A steam engine and carriages approaching Malvern Link, Malvern's first railway station, which opened in 1859*

During this period, many towns were provided with Corn Exchanges, where deals could be transacted in greater comfort than in the outdoor market place. At Worcester, after rival sites had been considered, a fine classical Corn Exchange was built in Angel Street in 1848, fronted by 'truly colossal' pairs of Tuscan columns. A similar venture at Droitwich led to a grand public opening in 1853 but the building closed after three months, allegedly because the farmers' wives preferred Worcester or Bromsgrove ,'where the drapers shops had a wider variety of goods'.

Communications

The early years of this period saw improvements in both water and road transport. In 1842 a Parliamentary Bill was passed to allow funds to be raised for the improvement of the Severn navigation. Locks were constructed almost at once at Bevere, Diglis, Holt and Lincombe, all within a few miles of Worcester, and others were built between 1843 and 1870. The locks made passage of the Severn less dependent on natural forces, and allowed the canal network, which fed into the river, to operate more efficiently. Road travel also improved, largely due to resurfacing by the Turnpike Trusts. The 1830s saw the apogee of the coaching era, and was the age of the 'flying coaches', such as the *Hibernia*, which in May 1832 did the run from Liverpool to Worcester in eleven hours six minutes.

It was the coming of the railway, however, which revolutionised travel in Worcestershire, as it did elsewhere. There had been schemes to link Birmingham to the Severn estuary from as early as 1824, but nothing came of them until 25 September 1835, when a joint committee of potential investors from Birmingham and Gloucester met at the *Star Hotel*, Worcester. Their proposals received the royal assent in April 1836 and the line from Cheltenham to Bromsgrove was opened on 24 June 1840. It was extended to outer Birmingham by December 1840, eight months later linking with the London-Birmingham railway, which had opened in 1838. The construction of the Gloucester-Birmingham line was an engineering triumph, for it had to ascend the Midlands plateau by the notorious Lickey Incline, still the steepest main line gradient in the British Isles. Due to reluctant landowners, however, this line bypassed Worcester, so that

106 *Malvern Link station on 25 July 1859, showing the first train to use the newly completed line to the outskirts of Worcester. The line was extended to Great Malvern by May 1860*

107 *Lickey Incline c.1840, a freight train of the period climbs towards Blackwell behind a Norris-built 2-4-0*

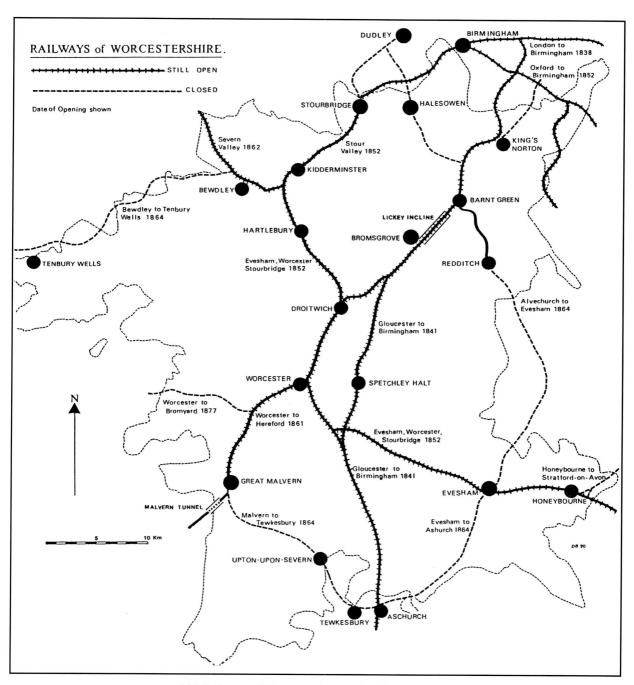

RAILWAYS of WORCESTERSHIRE.

———————————————— STILL OPEN

– – – – – – – – – – – – – – CLOSED

Date of Opening shown

DUDLEY

BIRMINGHAM

London to Birmingham 1838

Oxford to Birmingham 1852

STOURBRIDGE

HALESOWEN

KING'S NORTON

Severn Valley 1862

Stour Valley 1852

KIDDERMINSTER

BEWDLEY

BARNT GREEN

LICKEY INCLINE

Bewdley to Tenbury Wells 1864

HARTLEBURY

BROMSGROVE

REDDITCH

TENBURY WELLS

Evesham, Worcester Stourbridge 1852

Alvechurch to Evesham 1864

DROITWICH

Gloucester to Birmingham 1841

N

WORCESTER

SPETCHLEY HALT

Worcester to Bromyard 1877

Worcester to Hereford 1861

Evesham, Worcester, Stourbridge 1852

Gloucester to Birmingham 1841

Honeybourne to Stratford-on-Avon

GREAT MALVERN

EVESHAM

HONEYBOURNE

MALVERN TUNNEL

Malvern to Tewkesbury 1864

Evesham to Ashurch 1864

DB 90

5   10 Km

UPTON-UPON-SEVERN

TEWKESBURY

ASCHURCH

108 *Railways of Worcestershire in the 19th century*

109 *A Stourbridge glass epergne and a pair of vases, made about 1890*

110 *A superb vase and cover made in Worcester about 1820. It celebrates the glorious victory at Waterloo in 1815 and shows the meeting of Wellington and Blucher at the end of the battle*

until 1852, when a new line opened between Evesham, Worcester and Kidderminster, the county town was served only by a horse-drawn road omnibus, which met the train at Spetchley halt.

During the next 40 years, a network of railways sprawled across the county. Predictably, the density was greatest in the north, to serve the spawning industrial towns on and near the south Staffordshire coalfield, but a number of rural railways linked the market towns to the main lines, such as that running south-west from Evesham, serving the small villages of Ashton-under-Hill and Beckford, now within the county boundary, but then part of Gloucestershire. The arrival of the railway in a community was a great public occasion, as when the line from Kidderminster reached Tenbury Wells in 1864. The celebrations included a public breakfast in the field by the medieval castle motte, a carnival in the afternoon and a ball in the evening at the *Swan Hotel*. Everywhere the railway brought great changes, nowhere more so than at Great Malvern, where 3,000 visitors flooded into the town during the 12 months after the line from Worcester opened in 1861.

Manufacturing

Trade directories and census returns provide much firmer statistical information about manufacturing in this period than previously. Joseph Bentley's *Directory of Worcestershire*, published in 1841, has some 15,000 entries, 25 per cent of which relate to crafts and industries. About a third are concerned with 'ironwork, metals and heavy industries', which were concentrated in the north-east. Altogether, 134 trades are listed. Some of these had a number of firms, such as the 30 carpet manufacturers, mostly in Kidderminster, or the 138 needle and fishhook makers, nearly all in the Redditch area, but others had only a handful of practitioners, such as two organ-builders or two iron-boatmakers. The number of firms engaged in the distribution trades and the preparation of clothing and food was even greater, accounting for 35 per cent of Bentley's entries. These were all around the county, but with clusters in the areas of greatest population. Pigot's 1835 *Directory* lists more than 200 maltsters, with substantial numbers in the smaller market towns —12 in Upton-on-Severn, seven in Pershore, and even more in the larger centres— 31 at Worcester, 38 at Dudley and an amazing 60 at Stourbridge.

The extractive industries were part of the industrial base. Coal was mined in north Worcestershire, an extension of the south Staffordshire field, and in 1835 coal pits were described as 'very numerous around Stourbridge and Dudley', though few were deeper than 60 ft. The coal was soft and not suitable for many industrial purposes, but in the Dudley area production remained at about 700,000 tons for much of the period, employing some 2,500 persons. There was another field in the Forest of Wyre, but here the seams were thin and inferior. In the north-east local ironstone continued to be widely extracted, but this too was of generally low mineral content, and richer ores had to be brought in from elsewhere. In the Droitwich area large amounts of salt continued to be produced, with new pits being developed at Stoke Prior. The brine was extracted through copper rods from depths of about 200 ft., and was then piped to salt-pans, which were heated by great furnaces in order to remove the salt from its liquid, the salt being removed in great bars.

The iron-based industries of the north-east were characterised by the great variety of specialised products. In Dudley in 1835, the list of firms included seven anvil-makers, 12 chain-makers, 17 fender-makers, 18 fire iron-makers, 30 nail factors and 18 vice-makers. These obtained some of their materials from the 23 iron-founders and the 12 iron-masters, one of the latter, for example, being William Hoden, 'manufacturer of bar, roll and slit horse nail rods'. Stourbridge had its own specialities, including 11 'spade, shovel and edge tool manufacturers' and three manufacturers of 'steam engine boilers and gasometers'. In reality, many firms made a number of products and several are listed at least twice.

The china industry of Worcester, the glass industry of Stourbridge and the carpet industry of Kidderminster all continued to feed national and indeed international markets during this period, part of the great boom in production and in exports which characterised the Victorian age. They all experienced some technical and organisational changes, none more so than the carpet manufacturing of Kidderminster. In 1838 there were 24 manufacturers, who owned between them some 2,000 looms, most of which were lent to outworkers, who operated them in their own houses. Later in the century, however, it became more economical to gather the looms together into large factories, where they could be operated by steam power, as in the works erected in Gower Street by Lord Ward, later the Earl of Dudley.

111 *New Hawne Colliery, Halesowen*

From the 1830s the Worcester Royal Porcelain Company had to face competition from inferior wares and for a period had to discontinue the decorative porcelain on which its reputation was based. In the 1850s, however, ornamental ware revived, including 'biscuit porcelain', porcelain without a glaze, and this was used for a range of new products. These included a famous Worcester service depicting scenes from Shakespeare's *A Midsummer Night's Dream*.

A similar revolution occurred in the Worcester glove industry, which after 1832 made desperate attempts to withstand the competition of cheaper gloves from abroad. These even included an attempt in 1840 to persuade the young Queen Victoria to wear Worcester gloves and so revive the industry by a new fashion. This initiative failed, but others were more successful, and by 1851 the industry had some 2,500 employees, most of them gloveresses stitching cut leather in their homes. The next half century, however, saw the introduction of sewing

112 *A Dudley nailshop*

machines, and these too were assembled in factories, such as that of Messrs. Fownes in Talbot Street. In 1884 this firm was even described as having 'an army of teapots for the refreshment of the women employed at the sewing machines'.

Though on a much smaller scale than the urban-based industries, village craftsmen continued to make a significant contribution to the county's production during this period. In some places, specialist industries persisted, as at Belbroughton, where 39 men were still employed in scythe-making in 1851, or even in the parishes of the rural south, where, for example, the comparatively small parish of Cropthorne had a brick and tile manufacturer in 1860.

The Towns: variable fortunes

The number of town dwellers in Worcestershire increased considerably during this period, but the fortunes of individual towns varied enormously. Boundary changes, such as those following the Local Government Act of 1894, make precise comparisons across the period difficult, but broad patterns can be discerned. The smaller market towns, namely Alvechurch, Bewdley, Broadway,

Pershore, Tenbury and Upton-on-Severn, all had basically static totals, with the 1901 figures sometimes being less than those of 1831. Thus Broadway dropped from 1,517 to 1,414 and Pershore from 5,275 to 4,825. Bromsgrove, Droitwich and Evesham were more prosperous market towns, and in each case the population almost doubled, that of Bromsgrove, the largest of the three, rising from 8,612 to 14,096. At Worcester, the county town, the growth rate was about the same, from 27,641 to 49,790. Great Malvern, due to the successful promotion of the spa, achieved a much higher growth rate of four and a half times, from 4,150 to 19,131. The most spectacular increases, however, occurred in the north-east, where formerly distinct settlements now merged to form an almost continuously built-up area on the edge of Birmingham and the so-called Black Country further west. The largest growth of a town was at Halesowen, which rocketed from 9,765 to 38,868, making it almost as large as Dudley. Even more striking was the escalation in Yardley parish, rising from 2,488 in 1831 to 33,946 in 1901, as formerly separate townships like Sparkhill and Acock's Green were absorbed into the outward spread of Birmingham.

The Municipal Reform Act, which was passed in 1835 as part of the legislation which followed the Reform Act of 1832, made changes in the government of these towns. At Bewdley, Droitwich, Evesham, Kidderminster and Worcester self electing oligarchic corporations were replaced by mayors, aldermen and councillors, elected by the better-off male citizens. The process was sometimes resisted, as at Droitwich, where the town clerk conveyed the town hall site to himself and refused to surrender documents. Of the rest, the largest towns eventually became boroughs— Dudley in 1865, Stourbridge in 1914, but Halesowen not until 1936. The others became urban districts in their own right, as did Bromsgrove as a result of the Local Government Act of 1858, or were administered as part of a rural district, like Broadway, which became part of Evesham district.

The appearance of all these towns changed greatly during this period. Many town halls were rebuilt or remodelled, often using red brick, as at Stourbridge in 1887. Reflecting the civic gospel prevalent in Birmingham and other great cities, a number of improvements were made, such as the diversion at Bromsgrove of the stream which had previously flowed down the central street. Gas lighting was proudly installed in most towns, for example at Evesham in 1836 when it was claimed that 'by this means the dirt of candle ends and oil lamps has been happily eliminated from shops and offices'. A spate of libraries and institutes swept the county, especially late in the period, resulting in striking buildings of brick, terracotta and other fashionable materials, like the fine Victoria Institute in Foregate Street, Worcester. Public parks and gardens were an important part of the Victorian urban ethic. They can be found next to high density housing developments, as at Kidderminster, beside rivers as at Evesham or incorporating bandstands and pavilions as at Great Malvern. At Evesham, the gardens on both sides of the River Avon were created by removing osier beds and decayed wharves in a typically Victorian burst of town improvement. Like the new bridge completed in 1856, the gardens were named after the indefatigable Henry Workman, who was mayor many times. They were opened in 1864, with a grand Evesham flower show and regatta.

113 The Old Town Hall at Dudley, which was demolished in 1860 to 'improve' the town by creating more space in the market-place. It was replaced by a fountain donated by the Earl of Dudley

114 A view across the Workman gardens at Evesham, opened in 1864

Spas and watering places

Three Worcestershire towns—Tenbury, Great Malvern and Droitwich—all began or continued development as spas or watering places during this period. Mineral waters were found at Tenbury in 1839 and baths and a pump room were built within a year, the name of the town being changed to Tenbury Wells. Joseph Bentley, in his *History of Worcestershire*, published in 1840, predicted that 'this place is very likely to become of great importance', but in 1851 the population was only l,786, almost exactly what it had been in 1831. At Great Malvern, in contrast, where a spa was already well known, there was rapid expansion after 1842, when a young doctor, James Wilson, established it as a centre for hydropathic cures. These he had learnt at Graefenburg in Silesia from Vincenz Priessnitz, a pioneer of this kind of treatment. In spite of the discomforts involved—patients were woken at 5 a.m. and wrapped in a cold wet sheet for an hour—the treatment proved popular, and Great Malvern, with Malvern Link and Malvern Wells, grew rapidly between 1845 and 1861, with a number of large hotels going up, including the *Imperial* in 1860, later Malvern Girls' College. Other forms of treatment eventually came into favour but, even when their efficacy was questioned, Malvern thrived as a place for retirement, and late Victorian villas mushroomed over the hillsides. At Droitwich growth came later, and was largely due to the enterprise of John Corbett, who operated the salt works at Stoke Prior which were later called 'the most complete and compact in the world'. He used the profits to develop Droitwich as a spa, building Salters' Hall in 1881, opening the St Andrew's Brine Baths in 1887 and erecting a number of hotels. But Droitwich lacked the scenic delights of Malvern and there was no comparable boom in the property market.

Rural life

Throughout this period most rural parishes were still largely self-sufficient communities. Nearly every village had its own shop, often combined with a post-office, as in the small settlement at More in the Avon valley between Pershore and Evesham, part of the large parish of Fladbury. The proprietor was Esther Bullock, variously described in late 19th-century trade directories as post-mistress, provision dealer and licensed dealer in tobacco. Most villages had their local craftsmen, including the all-important blacksmith, who shoed horses and repaired farm implements. A recently published collection of old photographs from Upton Snodsbury, a few miles east of Worcester, catches the flavour of the village smithy with the caption 'You 'old to 'is 'ead and I'll 'ammer 'is 'off!'. In 1851 Cropthorne, a village on the Avon with 336 people, had a wheelwright as well as the blacksmith, and there were also six joiners and two carpenters, as well as a grocer, a butcher and two shoemakers. Rural corn mills were an integral part of the village economy, and a number of them can still be found, as at Grafton Flyford, a few miles east of Upton Snodsbury on the modern A422 to Stratford-on-Avon. Others, however, have long since gone, for example the Bant Mill at Stoke Heath near Bromsgrove, which was demolished in 1902. Another well-known village type was the day labourer, men such as 'honest John Tetsell' of Eastham, who owned two horses and a spring cart and transported fruit and coal in and around the parish.

115 *The exotic pump rooms at Tenbury Wells, built in 1840. They are now in a ruined condition and may have to be demolished*

Traditional village amusements were still widely enjoyed. At Beckford, for example, the ancient custom of Thomasing prevailed into the 20th century. On St Thomas's day, which was 21 December, the old women of the parish perambulated the village and appealed to the principal residents for charity, either in money or in kind. At Hartlebury, the village held a notorious Wake on the first Sunday after 25 July, the feast day of St James, to whom the church was dedicated. In the same village the maypole was dressed annually, not on the 1st but on 29 May.

The village pubs provided a focus for many communal activities. In 1851 John Noake, in his *Rambler in Worcestershire*, records the rivalry between two benefit societies in Hanley Castle, each based on one of the village inns, the *Hanley Quay* Club and the *Three Kings* Club. He records that:

116 *The* Three Kings Inn *at Hanley Castle*

> The days which they perambulate the village in all the associated grandeur of blue, crimson and gold, the streamers and buttonhole nosegays of their anniversary gatherings are purposely kept apart, from a dread of inability to adjust the question of precedence ... The Hanley Quay give their loyalty and their best coats an airing round the village on the day of the restoration of King Charles and the Three Kings on the feast of Whit Tuesday ...'.

Alcoholism was a considerable problem during the Victorian period. When the squire of Elmley Castle asked two of his labourers how much cider they drank in a day, he is reputed to have been given the reply: 'Sometimes we drink 16 pints and sometimes we drink a lot if we can get it'. The entries in trade directories and census returns show that sources of alcohol were widespread, the village of Hartlebury having eight public houses and nine beer houses in 1841. In later years the licensing magistrates became more stringent, as in 1908 when the *Vine Inn* at Catshill in the large parish of Bromsgrove was closed on the grounds that 11 public houses were not needed for the 2,200 local inhabitants.

The increasing popularity of organised games was one antidote to this and other undesirable activities. Football and cricket clubs were encouraged by the squire and the parson alike and were formed in many villages in the 1880s and 1890s. Late in the period a number of village halls were built, one of the finest being that at Overbury, on the southern slopes of Bredon Hill. This was provided in 1896 by the benevolent squire, Robert Martin, and was designed by the London-based architect, Norman Shaw, with neo-Tudor and Baroque features.

The Great House

The focus and heartbeat of nearly every rural parish was its great house. This was supported by an estate which usually embraced much of the parish, with some of the leading farmers as tenants. Many other inhabitants were employed directly, as servants in the house, gardeners in the grounds or gamekeepers in the park. With the family and their relatives, such houses were communities in their own right. At Hagley Hall, for instance, home of the cultured 4th Lord Lyttelton, the 1851 census reveals a family of 10: Lord Lyttelton, Lady Lyttelton, their four sons and three daughters, and also Lord Lyttelton's brother, William, who was rector of Hagley. The children's governess occupied an intermediate position and there were also 21 residential servants, listed in something close to rank order: butler, groom, housekeeper, nurse, cook, nursemaid, kitchenmaid, three housemaids, nursery maid, stillroom maid, dairy maid, three laundry maids, scullery maid,

117 *The Italianate interior of Hewell Grange, built by Bodley and Garner in 1884-91 for the Earl of Plymouth*

118 *This mid-Victorian photograph shows a Dudley family group clustered around the statue of Poseidon, which served as a fountain in the ornamental lake south of Witley Court. The central figure, framed by a parasol, is Georgina, Countess of Dudley*

119 *Witley Court, bought and extended by the Foley iron-making dynasty, was sold in 1837 to a member of the Ward family, whose wealth was also derived from Midlands manufacturing. This is a view of the Court in 1843, before it was enlarged in the 1860s*

doorman, servant of all work, stable boy and washerwoman. There were also a number of out-servants, living at the Lodge and elsewhere. On the night of the census, the household was swelled by Lord Lyttelton's mother-in-law, Lady Gwynne, her companion, and two more servants. Relatives and friends came and went with great frequency, one visitor being William Gladstone, the rising politician, whose wife was Lady Lyttelton's sister.

This period saw a final flourish of life on the grand scale, before it was swept away or at least curbed by the First World War and its aftermath. Nowhere is this better illustrated than at Witley Court, which the Foleys were forced to sell in 1837, much of their wealth having been dissipated by the 7th lord, Thomas Foley, an obese gambler nicknamed 'Lord Balloon'. The purchaser was William Humble Ward (1818-85), heir to the earldom and the industrial fortune of the Dudley family, who had been in the forefront of the Industrial Revolution, owning ironworks, coal mines and limestone quarries in the Dudley area. At first the house was let to tenants, the most illustrious being Queen Adelaide, the widow of King William IV. She entertained lavishly here from 1844-46, the guests including many of the royal heads of Europe. In the 1850s William Ward, now 1st Earl of

Dudley by a new creation, employed the architect Samuel Daukes greatly to extend and enhance the house. He refaced the whole building in cut stone and built the great crescent which links the garden front to a new, magnificent orangery. Here the lst Earl and his son continued to entertain in the grand manner, a frequent guest being the Prince of Wales. The Prince's pleasures included shooting in the huge park, where 25 full-time keepers were employed. Extravagant entertaining also occurred at Hewell Grange, where Lord Windsor put on a firework display for the Shah of Persia which included blowing up part of the old hall.

Many other great houses were rebuilt or extended at this time, the Gothic revival style being greatly favoured. One of the finest was at Madresfield Court, just outside Great Malvern, where an older core was refurbished 'in a spiky and theatrical' manner for the 4th Earl of Beauchamp, a member of the Lygon family for whom the original house was built in the 15th century. Here architectural styles proliferated, with the grand Great Hall being fitted up with a 15th-century minstrels' gallery imported from elsewhere. The chapel, in contrast, has an early 20th-century 'Arts and Crafts' interior, especially commissioned by the wife of the 7th Earl as a wedding present to her husband.

Notable houses elsewhere include the Italianate Bricklehampton Hall in the far south of the county, built for the Woodward family in 1848, and a number of Jacobean-style mansions, such as Astley Hall in the north-west, built in the 1830s for the Lea family. But perhaps the most remarkable 19th-century great house, and also one of the best known because it is now a hotel, is Chateau Impney outside Droitwich. This has been described as 'an extraordinary evocation of a Louis XIII chateau' set in the heart of Worcestershire. It was built for the salt magnate John Smith, who had a French wife, and for many embodies the energy of the successful Victorian entrepreneur.

Public worship and church building

For all the major churches, this period was a time of seriousness and energy. For the Church of England, much of this flowed from the High Anglican Oxford movement of the 1840s. From 1841 onwards, with the appointment of Hugh Pepys, the Bishops of Worcester were both holy men and good administrators, in both respects an apparent contrast to some of their predecessors. Both the High Church movement and the so-called evangelical movement encouraged new church buildings, and made deliberate efforts to extend the work of the church in the industrial north-east, where some incumbents now had huge populations to deal with. A notable step was the creation of a new diocese of Birmingham in 1905, with Dr. Gore, Bishop of Worcester since 1902, being translated to the new see.

Many new churches were built in the fashionable Gothic style, while others, including much of Worcester Cathedral, were heavily restored. The work of a number of late Victorian church architects is represented in the county. These include all but the Norman tower at St Laurence, Alvechurch (1859-61) and St Mary, Sedgeberrow (1867-68), both by William Butterfield; St Peter and St Paul at Upton-on-Severn (1878-79) by Arthur Bloomfield; and St Michael at Smethwick (1892) by A. E. Street. At Worcester Cathedral, where the 'surface of the exterior and many windows' are mid-Victorian, restoration was begun by A. E. Perkins and continued by Sir Giles Gilbert Scott.

The nonconformists filled in the network they had already created. A typical sequence is that at Pershore where the Broad Street Baptist church replaced a converted malthouse in 1841, itself being later masked by schoolrooms at the front of the medieval burgage plot. In the industrial areas especially there were large new chapels, such as those built in mid-century at Smethwick and Oldbury, both suburbs of Birmingham. The Baptist chapel in Sansome Walk, Worcester, rebuilt in 1863-64, was one of the first nonconformist chapels to look more like a church than a meeting house. Another distinctive building is the battlemented Salvation Army Fort at Newton Lane, Cradley, built in 1893.

The Catholic Emancipation Act of 1829 encouraged a number of new buildings, and the poverty apparent in much Roman Catholic architecture in England is less discernible in Worcestershire, always a strong area for that faith. One of their finest buildings is at Hanley Swan, south of Great Malvern. Here the church of Our Lady and St Alphonsus was designed in 1846 by Charles Hansom of hansom cab fame, using funds provided by the Hornyolds of Blackmore Park, descendants of Thomas Hornyold who had helped Charles II to escape after the Battle of Worcester in 1651.

120 *The Roman Catholic church at Hanley Swan, built in 1846*

Attempts to improve society: poor law reform and education

An attempt to find a nationwide solution for a widespread problem was first apparent with the new poor law, introduced in 1834. This compulsorily amalgamated parishes into unions to provide for the poor and established Boards of Guardians. There were 11 such unions in Worcestershire. One of these was that of 34 parishes centred on Pershore, which built a workhouse for 200 inmates on land provided by the Earl of Coventry. The building cost £3,575 2s. 2d., with each parish contributing in proportion to its population, the largest amount coming from Holy Cross, Pershore, which gave £527 9s. 6d. The minute books give harrowing glimpses of life in this grim institution. In 1837, for instance, Maria Tandy was put on bread and water for breaking a window, while stones were to be procured 'for the paupers to break until a handmill could be got'.

The system was still in force at the end of the period. In 1894, the number of paupers receiving relief in the 11 unions was 7,228. For one of those unions, based in Upton-on-Severn, it was reported that 'the thrifty and sober do wonderfully well on their small means ... but the intemperate and wasteful are often in difficulties'.

The provision of an improved education system, in contrast, was achieved piecemeal, rather than by a single piece of legislation. Until 1870 elementary education for the poor was provided by ancient endowments, such as that at Rushock just outside Worcester, where a William Norris left property in 1702 to

121 *The interior of St Kenelm's church, Romsley, as painted by A. E. Everitt before its restoration in 1849, when the box pews and 'three decker pulpit' were removed*

support a schoolteacher and '30 poor children'. In the 19th century other schools were started by voluntary bodies, especially the Church of England National Society. As a result of the 1870 Education Act, however, Education Boards were set up in areas where the existing provision was not sufficient for all children, for whom attendance became compulsory in the 1880s. Meanwhile, a number of ancient grammar schools, such as Prince Henry's Grammar School at Evesham or the Grammar School at Halesowen, were brought under schemes of reformed management, while as a result of the 1902 Education Act a number of new secondary schools were provided by local authorities, such as Stourbridge Girls' Secondary School which opened in 1905. This period also saw the foundation of a number of independent schools, including St Michael's College, Tenbury, founded in 1856 by the Vicar of Tenbury for specialist church musical education; and Malvern College which opened in 1865 'for the education of the sons of gentlemen'. Another strand led through the Mechanics' Institutes of the 1830s and 1840s to technical institutions like the School of Art and Science which was built in Sansome Walk, Worcester, in the 1890s.

Sport, recreation and culture

At the beginning of the period ancient festivals were still widely observed as they had been since the Middle Ages. At Hartlebury, for instance, the ceremony of dressing the maypole took place annually on 29 May while on the first Sunday after 25 July the village had its Wake, a merrymaking which commemorated the dedication of the church to St James. Later in the century, however, organised team games grew in popularity, often encouraged by local squires and clergymen who had been brought up in their public schools to the new fashion for 'muscular Christianity'. Collections of early photographs invariably include late Victorian footballers and cricketers, for example Bromsgrove cricket club in 1909.

By the early 20th century, the improvement in communications was making Bank Holiday excursions to the countryside a popular activity. The gift by the Cadbury family of a portion of the Lickey Hills to the City of Birmingham provided one welcome outlet for this form of recreation. The more affluent and adventurous travelled further afield, to the Clent Hills or to the Malverns. Before the end of the 19th century packed trainloads of Worcestershire people departed each summer for the burgeoning seaside resorts, with Weston-super-Mare the most popular venue.

Higher up the social scale, the rich had their own diversions. There were a number of fox hound packs, usually led by great landlords, for example members of the Coventry family, who hunted the so-called Croom country in south-west Worcestershire from 1872. As early as 1837 there were racecourses at Dudley, Stourbridge, Tenbury, Upton-on-Severn and Worcester, and, though most did not survive very long, the Worcester Races, held on what was once the commonground of Pitchcroft on the banks of the Severn, close to the city centre, have always been popular.

For those with more cultural tastes, a number of societies were formed in the major towns, but none more successfully than at Malvern, where many well educated people were in retirement. New Assembly Rooms, built in 1884,

122 Edward Elgar, rated as England's finest composer since Purcell

attracted plays, lectures and penny readings, and a wide range of concerts, including personalities such as Jenny Lind, Albert Chevalier and Marie Lloyd. It was this kind of environment, perhaps, which helped to attract Edward Elgar, a native of Worcestershire and already a reputable musician, to settle in Malvern after his marriage in 1889. During a 14-year stay he composed two of his major works, *The Dream of Gerontius* and *Enigma Variations*. The latter in particular has come to be regarded as an idyll of the Worcestershire countryside and is sometimes thought of as the theme music of the county.

123 *A medallion won by Joseph Gilbert of Evesham, a patentee of agricultural implements in 1873. It was awarded by the Worcestershire Agricultural Society*

National and local identity

This was an age of patriotism, when English people became more conscious than previously of the British Empire. Rising population at home was reflected in increasing rates of immigration from all parts of the county, and was one underlying reason for Britain's imperialist policies. Worcestershire men and women served and worked in all parts of the expanding empire, often dying abroad, as did Viscount Windsor of Hewell Grange, Tardebigge, who died in India in 1909 from a fever, whilst acting as aide-de-camp to the Viceroy. A typical Victorian hero was young Marcus Cheek, the 17-year-old son of the town clerk of Evesham, who was captured and injured when the native garrison rebelled at Allahabad at the start of the Indian mutiny. His wounds were mortal but before dying he found the energy to rally an Indian Christian under torture with the words, 'Come what may, do not deny the Lord Jesus Christ'. Battalions of the Worcestershire Regiment, which had been founded in 1694, fought in the Sikh Wars of the 1840s, a third of the men involved dying in one action. The 5th and 6th battalions of this regiment were formed in 1900 to fight in South Africa in the Boer War and were entertained at a dinner in the Shire Hall on their return.

National patriotism was matched by greater local identity during this period. County societies such as the Worcestershire Agricultural Society and the Worcestershire Horticultural and Floral Society had been founded in 1817 and 1828 respectively but their annual shows only became major events after 1850, and were regarded as prestige occasions for the county. As spectator sports grew in popularity, Worcestershire County Cricket club won the Minor Counties Competition in 1896 and was admitted as a first class county in 1899. The early results were not spectacular, however, and before 1914 the county was so reliant on members of the Foster family—at one time seven members played for the county side—that it was sometimes nicknamed 'Fostershire'.

The most significant development was the formation of Worcestershire County Council in 1889, following the Local Government Act passed the previous year, and its gradual assumption of a number of county-wide responsibilities, including roads and some forms of education. This was matched in 1894 by the creation of a new structure of local government. As a result of the two acts, the largest urban areas, Worcester and Dudley, were recognised as county boroughs, two of 61 such boroughs in England and Wales. In addition, there were 12 municipal boroughs and urban districts, and eight rural districts, which took on a range of local responsibilities, ranging from the regulation of health standards to the provision of council houses.

Chapter 10

Modern Worcestershire: 1914-1990

Population and administration

124 *Map of administrative units in Hereford and Worcester County after 1974*

Even before the absorption of Worcestershire into the new county of Hereford and Worcester in 1974, there were a number of boundary changes affecting the county, especially in the north-east. Parts of Stourbridge in 1914 and Halesowen in 1936 were merged with the county borough of Dudley, and so were lost to Worcestershire. On the other hand, Oldbury, one of the Worcestershire municipal districts

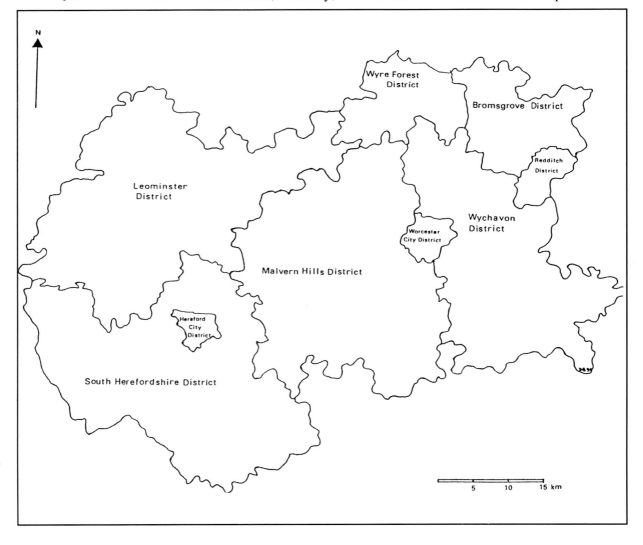

recognised in 1894, together with adjoining areas of Staffordshire, became the new County Borough of Warley in 1966. Halesowen, Stourbridge and Warley were all ceded to the new West Midlands Metropolitan County in 1974, the first two becoming part of Dudley and Warley part of Sandwell.

Population figures given in the census reports for Worcestershire relate to the administrative county and to the county boroughs of Worcester and Warley. Though not exactly comparable because of the changes affecting the north-east, they show a steady increase from the 380,483 of 1911 to a figure nearly twice as great, 693,253, in 1971. Comparisons between 1971 and 1981 cannot be made because of the boundary changes already described, but the population of Hereford and Worcester County in 1981 was 631,756, a rise of 12.8 per cent over 1971, which suggests that the pre-1971 population increase was being maintained.

In 1961, the density of population varied considerably across the county. The two county boroughs—Worcester and Warley—and the three municipal boroughs —Halesowen, Kidderminster and Stourbridge—all had more than 10 people to the acre, the most dense being Warley with 42. Precise comparisons between the seven urban districts of Bromsgrove, Droitwich, Evesham, Malvern, Redditch and Stourport-on-Severn, and the municipal borough of Bewdley, are not meaningful, because of the different amount of 'non-urban' land included within the administrative boundaries, but all had densities between 8.65 (Evesham) and 15.40 (Droitwich).

Of the eight rural districts, the highest density was that of Bromsgrove, with two persons a hectare, a reflection of the generally thicker settlement pattern in the north-east of the county. All the others had densities of less than one, the most marked difference being between those along the western edge of the county— Martley, Tenbury and Upton-on-Severn—all of which had densities of 0.74 or less; and those elsewhere, such as Droitwich, Evesham, Kidderminster and Pershore, which were between 0.96 and 0.74.

The Economy: Agriculture, Manufacturing and Servicing

For the whole of this period, the proportion of the population in paid employment has been about two-fifths. It rose just above this at times of national high employment, as in the 1960s. At other times it dropped a little below, especially in the 1930s, though the county was spared the horrors of mass unemployment except in parts of the industrial north-east. During the period a growing number of women took jobs outside the home, though in 1980 the number of men in full time employment was still more than twice the number of women.

In 1931, two-fifths of the workforce in Worcestershire were employed in manufacturing, compared with less than a tenth in agriculture, the county's traditional industry. The service industries, however, including transport, finance and administration, were already the largest group, accounting for 45 per cent of those in full time employment. In 1980, in the new county of Hereford and Worcester, the number of people employed in manufacturing had shrunk to only just over a quarter, and barely five per cent were engaged in agriculture, but those in the service industries had soared to more than three-fifths of the total. Another trend has been the growing number of people travelling considerable distances to

125 *Glass cones called cloches which were used in the Vale of Evesham for forcing crops, in order to get them to market as soon as possible*

work, often crossing county boundaries in the process. Of nearly 23,000 persons resident in Halesowen in 1961, for example, nearly half worked outside the municipal borough boundary, including some 5,000 who commuted into Birmingham.

Although agriculture employs a shrinking workforce, it has remained the principal form of land use, especially in the south of the county. A study published in 1947 showed that Worcestershire had ribbons of high quality category I land along the valleys of the Avon, Severn and Teme, and very little low quality category III land, except on the steeper slopes of the Malverns. In recent decades, the widespread availability of fertilisers has increased yields, while farming has become increasingly mechanised, with many farms amalgamating to form bigger units to achieve 'economies of scale'. A typical enterprise of this kind is that of the Holland-Martin family on the south side of Bredon Hill, which operates as Overbury Farms. An estate of some 5,000 acres has about half the land in crops, including 580 acres of oilseed rape and 100 acres of sugar beet. A pedigree herd of Guernsey cattle, a flock of 850 ewes, and some 400 Herefords reared for beef are supported on 560 acres of pasture and by a number of fodder crops. There is also a stud farm, which has produced some notable horses since 1950, including Grundy who won the Derby in 1975. A proportion of the land is commercial woodland. The estate is served by extensive irrigation, drawing upon a number of hillside reservoirs.

The production of hops, especially in the Teme valley, remained important for most of this period, though in recent years it has suffered from changes in the brewing process, and in the influx of lagers and other imported drinks. Until about 1950 the autumn hop-picking attracted gypsies and other casuals as well as children and mothers flooding out from adjoining towns. One farm at Eastham was serviced largely by pickers from the Black Country and used tally sticks to record the amount picked.

Fruit-farming and market-gardening have remained the most distinctive agricultural activities, especially in the Vale of Evesham. A recent guidebook has described the Vale as 'glorious with blossom in spring-time', and later in the year as 'colourful with yellow egg-plums, Prolifics, purple Pershores and Victorias'. The area is said to produce the world's finest asparagus, as well as strawberries, lettuce, radish, sprouts, cabbage, spring onions, peas and runner beans. This has been one branch of farming where the smallholder can survive. In 1967 an Elmley Castle horticulturalist is on record as having a 16-acre market garden on which he planted six acres of sprouts, as well as lesser amounts of beetroot, broad beans, lettuce, onions, parsley and spring cabbage.

In 1931 the largest industries were metals and engineering, which employed over 40,000 workers, well over half of them in Dudley, Halesowen, Oldbury and Stourbridge. The second largest category was textiles, which employed some 10,000 people, most of them in the carpet factories of Kidderminster. Since that date some traditional industries, such as Worcester's glove making, have declined, but others have achieved new reputations, as such with crystal glass manufacture at Stourbridge or Royal Worcester porcelain. The latter has benefited from new lines such as figure-modelling, which began with a pair of porcelain birds designed in 1935. At Redditch, new metal trades such as aluminium alloys have been added

126 During this period the tractor had almost completely ousted the horse for driving farm machinery

to the traditional manufacture of needles, fish-hooks and springs. Bromsgrove has one of the largest forging plants in Europe and Kidderminster one of the most modern drop forges.

Many industries are still tied to local agricultural produce, for example the manufacture of Worcester Sauce in Worcester itself, or the huge sugar beet factory on the Foley Industrial Estate just outside Kidderminster. Stourport has a long established vinegar works, while canning and egg packing are important at Evesham. An enterprise of a different kind is that represented by Worcester's 'House of Kays', one of the largest mail-order firms in the world.

127 *A Second World War tank outside Jeffries grocery shop in Bromsgrove*

The World Wars and their aftermath

In both the First and the Second World Wars, county regiments were involved in many historic actions. In 1915, the 2nd battalion of the Worcestershire Regiment made a gallant charge at Gheluvelt during the Battle of Ypres, which had a decisive effect on the outcome of that crucial engagement, halting the Germans in their advance to the English channel. For this action the Worcesters were especially cited by Elgar in the dedication of *The Spirit of England* to 'the glorious dead'; while after the war the battle gave its name to Worcester's 'Gheluvelt Park'. In the Second World War the Regiment fought bravely at Tobruk in North Africa, where heavy losses were sustained. In 1944, they were among the follow-up troops in Normandy and were among the first to cross the Rhine the following March. Another battalion of the Regiment fought in India and Burma and in 1945 took part in the capture of Mandalay. The Worcestershire Yeomanry, a territorial regiment, were present at Gallipoli in 1915 and the following year suffered heavy losses against the Turks in Palestine. In 1940 they were some of those who fought the rearguard action at Dunkirk, and they were among the first to return to France in 1944, going in by glider on 'D'-day to support the British 6th Airborne Division who had seized the bridgehead over the River Orne, on the east flank of the landing area.

As elsewhere, attitudes to war changed during the First World War. There was great flag waving and cheering at first, as at Evesham on 5 August 1914, when local volunteers marched from the Drill Hall in Coronation Street to the railway station. The mood was more sombre seven years later when the Earl of Coventry unveiled Evesham's war memorial in Abbey Park, with its grim list of over 200 dead. The county produced many heroes, such as Private Fred Dancox, from a deprived part of Worcester, who won a Victoria Cross in 1917; or the army chaplain, Geoffrey Studdert-Kennedy, who won the Military Cross, but thought it fitting to observe that 'real war is the final limit of damnable brutality—it's about the silliest, most unhumanely fatuous thing that ever happened'.

Both wars had tremendous impact on the life of ordinary Worcestershire people. Many women took jobs for the first time and in 1939 the south Worcestershire countryside was flooded with evacuees. Food shortages affected everyone and queueing became a part of everyday life. The county was more intensively cultivated than ever before and many great houses were turned into hospitals for wounded troops, for example Ballenhall Manor in the First World War, formerly the home of the Allsopps, the brewing magnates. The role of women in the war effort was considerable and nurses took part in Worcester's Victory Parade, led by the redoubtable Miss Diana Ogilvy, who became Mayor of Worcester in 1932.

In the Second World War, Worcestershire experienced some bombing, for example, of the Meco Works in Worcester on the night of 3 October 1940, which killed seven persons and wounded 64; but compared with Birmingham, just across the county boundary, casualties were light. Worcestershire had 12 battalions of the Home Guard and many other voluntary organisations were involved, as when the W.R.V.S. was asked to stand by in June 1940 to receive survivors from Dunkirk. Many of the county's factories were involved in war work, manufacturing items as diverse as artillery barrels and frames for Wellington bombers. Employment boomed and a number of new works were attracted to Worcestershire, including the Government's Telecommunications Research Establishment, which migrated to Great Malvern in 1942. Another migrant, in this case temporary, was the BBC, which moved to Wood Norton outside Evesham, a name that was changed to 'Hog's Norton' in a popular wartime radio show.

Perhaps more than any previous events in the county's history, the World Wars had the effect of widening the horizons of Worcestershire people. Young men and women, some of them from small towns and remote rural communities, found themselves transported to distant places. Some served with the county regiments in the Middle East, India or North Africa, while others travelled widely with the Royal Navy or trained in Canada with the R.A.F. Many of those who remained at home were thrust into new work or new forms of public service, while others formed liaisons with the American troops who were billeted at Hallow or at Blackmore Camp near Malvern. After the Second World War, there were 130 Worcestershire girls among the G.I. brides who crossed the Atlantic, but even among the rest of the population the impact of America's wartime culture was far-reaching.

128 An escalator linking floors at the Cornbow shopping precinct, Halesowen

The new horizons and the heightened aspirations of wartime accelerated processes of social change which are rooted in the events of the 19th century and earlier. In 1928, the goal of universal adult suffrage was attained when all women were allowed to vote. The Beveridge Report of 1942 and the Education Act of 1944 were major landmarks that helped to set the framework for post-war society, in Worcestershire as elsewhere. Food rationing and other shortages persisted for nearly a decade after the end of the Second World War but the coronation of Queen Elizabeth II in 1953, celebrated with great joy in nearly every Worcestershire town and village, ushered in an age of unprecedented material prosperity. This was first generally appreciated in the late 1950s and early 1960s, when politicians claimed that 'you've never had it so good'. By 1970, there was one private motor vehicle in Worcestershire for every three and a half people, while a high proportion of homes enjoyed central heating, television, refrigeration and a range of other appliances.

The central and regional controls needed in wartime had conditioned people to accept a greater degree of planning, the case for which had been gathering momentum since the 19th century. The 1947 Town and Country Planning Act constituted city and district councils as local planning authorities and this and later acts gave them an increasing range of powers.

129 *The older parts of Hanley Castle High School, which is now a comprehensive school serving a large rural area. The school began as a Grammar School in 1544, and was extended several times in the 19th and 20th centuries*

130 *Victoria Square, Droitwich, one of many areas once open to traffic which have been pedestrianised in recent years. In the distance is the Raven Hotel, parts of which are 16th-century, but which was extended in the 1880s by John Corbett, the salt magnate who developed Droitwich as a fashionable spa*

131 *A factory at Stoke Prior, landscaped in a rural setting*

132 *Farm buildings at Upper House, Alfrick, recently converted into residences, and now called Crews Hill. From left to right the buildings were once a milking parlour, the original farmhouse a stable range, an oasthouse and a barn. Oasthouses were once common in north-west Worcestershire but nearly all are now redundant or converted*

Adapting old towns and creating new

The largely uncontrolled outward growth of cities and towns, which was one justification for the 1947 Act, was apparent all over Worcestershire. The population of every town increased, sometimes dramatically, as at Bromsgrove, which grew from 14,096 in 1901 to 34,497 in 1961. By 1961 Worcester City had a population of 65,923, while Halesowen, Kidderminster and Stourbridge all had just over 45,000. The clearance of areas of poor quality, often insanitary housing and the provision of large new estates of council housing were among the greatest achievements of the new local authorities. In Worcester between 1936 and 1939, for example, 846 houses were demolished or closed, 132 were 'made fit', while 753 council houses were built. Private houses were also built, often on the edge of towns as 'ribbon development' along main roads, for example, the A456 outside Hagley.

The reconciliation of the needs of pedestrians and the ever increasing number of vehicles was a major concern of planners, especially in the larger towns. Bypasses have been built at Bromsgrove, Halesowen and Bewdley, and ring-roads at Stourbridge and Kidderminster. The necessity for measures of this kind is accepted by nearly everyone but the details have often been criticised, an example being the routing of the Kidderminster ring road between St Mary's church and Church Street leading up to it. The creation of a fast-traffic through road in front of the cathedral at Worcester showed a similar lack of architectural sensitivity and has been criticised as an 'incomprehensible ... act of self-mutilation'.

Pedestrianisation schemes have been a feature of post-war town planning. Examples include the high streets at Bromsgrove and Worcester, while a very recent scheme is that adjoining the Booth Hall in Evesham, a delightful re-creation of the opportunity to 'walk-about' in part of the traditional market-place. Shopping developments have been another innovation of recent years. The Cornbow Development at Halesowen, with an enclosed precinct on two levels, is an adaptation of the trading complex which has infilled the original triangular market-place since the Middle Ages, and provides a major shopping facility close to an encircling road and a bus station. A smaller, but equally sensitive development, is that behind the former *Royal Three Tuns Hotel* in Pershore, where the newly created Royal arcade accommodates nine small shops.

The most ambitious planned development has been that at Redditch, which was designated a New Town in 1964, with a target population of 70,000 within 20 years. Blessed with easy access from adjoining motorways, Redditch has what has been called 'a superlative road system', though this has led to the quip that it is easier to bypass Redditch than to find. The town has a number of self-contained 'neighbourhoods', which have been sensitively tailored to the undulating landscape, leaving the high land free of buildings. A plan to create a new shopping centre was abandoned but the old centre has been greatly expanded and enhanced, and has so many trees and plants that it has been nicknamed 'Palm Court'.

The Changing Countryside

With the development of country bus services and wider ownership of private cars, the level of rural isolation was considerably reduced in the years before 1939. A survey in 1945 of shopping and entertainment patterns in central and south

133 *Palm Court shopping precinct at Redditch New Town*

Worcestershire showed that most villages looked to Worcester as their major regional centre, though Evesham and Redditch were local centres largely outside the influence of the county town. For cinema and shopping, many people looked to nearer centres, such as Droitwich, Malvern, Pershore and Upton-on-Severn.

In the post-war years, the decline in the number of persons employed in agriculture, combined with a greater general affluence and the increase in the number of private cars, has brought many changes to rural life. In some areas, population has declined, for example in the small parish of Netherton, a few miles south-west of Evesham, where there were 55 residents in 1951 but only 31 in 1981. Elsewhere, however, the population has soared, partly due to people coming into the countryside from the towns and conurbations, either to retire or to commute. At Chaddesley Corbett, for example, nearly every house in the main street is now occupied by professional families from Birmingham or further afield, or by retired people. At Elmley Castle, the population has risen from 310 in 1951 to 468 in 1981, and a recent study has shown that 'the village ... is gradually changing from being a community of families, inter-related by blood, to a community of families who have come in during the past forty years ...'. Paradoxically, this process has increased the isolation of families without cars, for demand is no longer sufficient to sustain many local bus services. As shown by a recent study in Hereford diocese, which includes the north-west of the old county of Worcestershire, this kind of isolation is only one factor which causes real and widespread rural deprivation, affecting perhaps a quarter of rural residents.

134 *The village street at Chaddesley Corbett, now largely a dormitory village*

One loss to many rural parishes has been a resident Church of England clergyman. Many parishes now share one vicar or are part of a group of parishes served by a team of clergy. The church authorities urge the need for new kinds of lay ministry, but many country people lament the demise of the local parson. In some villages, a long line of local squires has also come to an end. In Elmley Castle, for example, the manor house has fallen into ruin since the death of Sir Francis Davies in 1948, a distinguished soldier who, it is said, knew every family personally. In Worcestershire, first schools have been retained in as many villages as possible, but the school bus taking children to middle and high schools is now a regular part of rural life. The county is rightly proud of its rural high schools, for example that at Hanley Castle, incorporating a grammar school which goes back to the 16th century or earlier.

A number of bodies, including English Heritage and the National Trust, maintain historic properties in the Worcestershire countryside and open them to the public. The Avoncroft Museum of Buildings, just outside Bromsgrove, has preserved and rebuilt a number of buildings from both inside and outside the county. Those from Worcestershire include an 18th-century barn from Temple Broughton near Hanbury. The work of preserving the countryside has been helped by the Worcestershire Nature Conservation Trust, which was formed as a registered charity in 1968. It now manages 59 sites spread over 1,500 acres, one such site being Tiddesley Wood, a mile west of Pershore, which is noted for its orchids and nightingales. In the towns, similar work is performed by local Civic Societies, who are sometimes caught up in contentious planning matters, such as the proposal, which was ultimately successful, to create a commercial marina at Upton-on-Severn.

135 *One of the early omnibuses which linked Worcestershire villages and market towns in the early 1920s*

136 Harry Oakes and
Gwen Berryman
playing Dan and
Doris Archer in 1957

An unusual but effective vehicle for the promotion of rural matters and concerns has been the long-running BBC radio serial, *The Archers*, which started on 1 January 1951. Ambridge, in and around which the serial is set, is a composite of a number of Worcestershire villages. The *Bull*, where so much village business is transacted, is supposedly modelled on the fine timber-framed inn of that name in Inkberrow. The marriage of Philip Archer and Grace Fairbrother, which gripped the nation's attention in 1955, took place in St Mary's, Hanbury. But the Laky Hill up which the characters occasionally climb, for reflection or solitude, is surely Bredon Hill, and Ashton-under-Hill is regarded by many as the real prototype for Ambridge. The programme has helped to increase public awareness of a number of rural issues, as in 1956, when Dan Archer's cattle herd had to be destroyed, and many townspeople realised for the first time the enormity of foot-and-mouth disease.

Administration and Future Planning

The 1974 changes created a new county, Hereford and Worcester, of nine administrative units, five of which—Bromsgrove, Redditch, Wychavon, Wyre Forest and Worcester City—came entirely from what had been Worcestershire, while two others, Leominster and Malvern Hills, were carved from both the former counties. In 1989, all the units totally in the former area of Worcestershire had populations of more than 75,000, while the units totally in what had been Herefordshire all had less than 50,000.

A County Structure Plan to provide a framework for future development was issued in 1985 and revised in 1988. The plan which accompanied it is reproduced in a simplified form as Fig.137. It is a convenient peg on which to hang descriptions of communications and other matters, as they are at the end of the long period covered in this book.

The most important line of communication in the county is undoubtedly the M5, which was built in the 1960s, unfortunately with only two lanes along most of its length through Worcestershire. Parts of this have been widened and otherwise improved in recent years. Its offshoot, the M50 to South Wales, cuts through the far south-west of what was formerly Worcestershire, while the M42, which links to the M6, runs east from Bromsgrove, and now interchanges with the M5 at Catshill. Two spaciously laid out service stations, at Strensham in the south and Frankley in the north, provide much the same function for the fast-moving travellers of today as coaching inns like the *George* at Bewdley or the *Angel* at Pershore did for their 18th-century predecessors.

As shown on Fig.137, a number of primary A roads, known as National Regional Distributor roads, fill out the basic motorway network. Eight of these converge on Worcester, most of them following very ancient routeways, while others cross outlying sectors of the county, especially in the south-east and the crowded north-east. A number of railways remain in use, though the rural north-west is totally devoid of this form of transport.

Fig. 137 shows that the Malverns, Bredon Hill and the Worcestershire portion of the Cotswolds near Broadway have been classed as Areas of Outstanding Natural Beauty. The whole of the north-east, together with a smaller area between

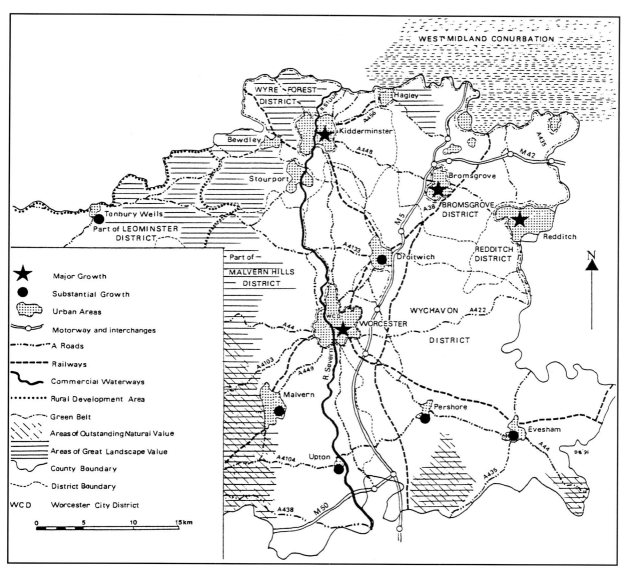

Droitwich and Worcester, has been designated as part of a Green Belt, fringing the Birmingham and West Midlands conurbation. Here, very strict planning controls are exercised, allowing development for only essential economic need. The far north-west, in and around the Teme Valley, is a Rural Development Area, where there are incentives for business ventures and community enterprises. Both here and in the rest of the county, small scale developments can be permitted by the district councils. Another kind of development is the conversion of redundant barns and other farm buildings, many of which have been undertaken in Worcestershire, for this is considered to be a way of providing homes in rural areas without scattering new buildings around the countryside.

137 Diagrammatic map showing some aspects of the Hereford and Worcester County structure plan, 1988

Fig.137 shows that considerable expansion is still planned for Worcestershire, with major areas of growth at Kidderminster, Bromsgrove and Redditch, all of them in pockets within the Green Belt; and also at Worcester, where in 1986 it was planned to build some 6,000 new dwellings before 2001. Substantial growth is also planned for Droitwich, with lesser developments at Evesham, Malvern, Pershore, Tenbury and Upton-on-Severn.

What 'Worcestershire' means

Administratively, Worcestershire is a lost county, but for many people, not all of them local residents, the term is still emotive and meaningful. For some, Worcestershire means the County Cricket Club, which has thrived greatly in recent years, winning the John Player League in 1971, 1987 and 1988, and the County Championship in 1989. For others, it means prestigious arts events, particularly the Malvern Festival, founded by Sir Barry Jackson in 1929, when G. B. Shaw's new play, *The Apple Cart* , was the main attraction; or the Three Choirs Festival held every third year at Worcester, as in August 1990, when the 263rd annual meeting was held. For others again, it means weekend drives along the Blossom route in the Teme valley, bracing hikes over the Malverns or serene cruises up and down the Avon or the Severn.

To the historian, however, Worcestershire is a palimpsest of many millennia, formed and shaped by momentous natural forces, and then scratched and nibbled by the hand of man. The landscape of today, threaded by motorways and argued over by planners and conservationists, is the end product of centuries of human toil. From knowledge of the past may come wisdom for the future—and towards that end it is hoped that this slim volume will make a slight contribution.

Bibliography

Belbroughton History Society, Belbroughton: *Aspects of the history of Belbroughton in the 18th and 19th centuries* (Belbroughton, 1981)

Bond, C. J., 'The Topography of Pershore', in the Vale of Evesham Historical Society Research Papers, No. 6 (Evesham, 1977)

British Association for the Advancement of Science, *Birmingham and its Regional Setting* (Birmingham, 1950)

Burton, J. R., *A History of Bewdley* (London, 1883)

Carver, M. O. H., *Medieval Worcester: Reports, Surveys, Texts and Essays* (Worcester, 1980)

Chaddesley Corbett Local History Group, *Work in Progress* (Chaddesley Corbett, 1982)

Cox, B. G. and Alcock, D. G., *Yesterday's Town: Evesham* (Buckingham, 1979)

Cox, D. C., 'The Vale Estate of the Church of Evesham, *c*.700-1086', Vale of Evesham Historical Society Research papers, Vol. 5 (Evesham, 1975)

Darby, H. C. and Terrett, I. B., *The Domesday Geography of Midland England* (Cambridge, 1954)

Davies, V. L. and Hyde, H., *Dudley and the Black Country 1760 to 1860* (Dudley, 1970)

Dodd, J. P., *Worcestershire Agriculture in the mid-nineteenth century* (Worcester, 1979)

Dreghorn, W., *Geology Explained in the Severn Vale and Cotswolds* (Newton Abbot, 1967)

Dyer, A., *The City of Worcester in the sixteenth century* (Leicester, 1973)

Dyer, C., *Lords and Peasants in a Changing Society* (Cambridge, 1980)

Finberg, H. P. R., *The Early Charters of the West Midlands* (Leicester, 1961)

Gait, R. C., *A History of Worcestershire Agriculture and Rural Evolution* (1939)

Glaisyer, J., and others, *County Town: A Civic Survey for the Planning of Worcester* (London, 1946)

Hereford and Worcester County Council, *Structure Plan; Written Statement* (Worcester, 1985)

Hereford and Worcester County Council, *Alterations to the Written Statement and Explanatory Memorandum* (Worcester, 1988)

Hickin, N. B., *Wyre Forest Refreshed* (Kidderminster, 1981)

Hilton, R. H., *A Medieval Society: the West Midlands at the end of the thirteenth century* (Cambridge, 1966)

Hooke, D., *The Anglo-Saxon Landscape: the Kingdom of the Hwicce* (Manchester, 1985)

Hughes, P. and Molyneux, N., *Worcester Streets: Friar Street* (Worcester, 1984)

Hughes, P., *Worcester Streets: Blackfriars* (Worcester, 1986)

Humphries, J., *Studies on Worcestershire History* (Birmingham, 1938)

Hurle, P., *Hanley Castle, Heart of Malvern Chase* (Chichester, 1978)

Hurle, P., *Upton: Portrait of a Severnside Town* (Chichester, 1979)

Hurle, P., *The Abbey Gateway, Malvern* (Malvern, 1986)

Jones, M., *Maps of Birmingham* (Birmingham, 1975)

Kissack, K., *The River Severn* (Lavenham, 1982)

Large, P., 'Urban growth and agricultural change in the West Midlands during the seventeenth and eighteenth centuries', in Clark, P., *The Transformation of English Provincial Towns 1600-1800* (London, 1984)

Lloyd, Rev. R. H., *Bredon Hill and its Villages* (Evesham, 1987)

Lyes, D. C., *The Leather Glove Industry of Worcester in the Nineteenth Century* (Worcester, 1973)

Nash, T., *Collections for the History of Worcestershire* (1781/82)

Oppitz, L., *Hereford and Worcester Railways Remembered* (Newbury, 1990)

Peacock, R., *Hagley from the Sixteenth to the Nineteenth Century* (Hagley, 1985)

Pevsner, N., *The Buildings of England: Worcestershire* (London, 1968)

Richards, A. and S., *The Byegone Bromsgrove Picture Book* (Bromsgrove, 1983)

Rollins, J. G., *A History of Redditch* (Chichester, 1984)

Rowlands, M. B., *Masters and Men in the West Midlands metalware trades before the industrial revolution* (Manchester, 1975)

Royal Commission: *The Historical Monuments of England. Nonconformist Chapels and Meeting-houses: Herefordshire, Worcestershire and Warwickshire* (London, 1986)

Salter, M., *The Castles of Herefordshire and Worcestershire* (Wolverhampton, 1989)

Sherwood, R. B., *Civil Strife in the Midlands* (Chichester, 1974)

Skipp, V., *Medieval Yardley* (Chichester, 1970)

Skipp, V., *Crisis and Development: An Ecological Case Study of the Forest of Arden 1570-1674* (Cambridge, 1978)

Slater, T. and Jarvis, P. J., *Field and Forest: An historical geography of Warwickshire and Worcestershire* (Norwich, 1982)

Smith, B. C., *A History of Malvern* (Malvern, 1978)

Smith, L. D., *Carpet Weavers and Carpet Masters: the hand loom carpet weavers of Kidderminster 1780-1850* (Kidderminster, 1986)

Smith, T. S., *Leland's Itinerary in England and Wales* (London, 1964)

Stephenson, J., *Florence of Worcester: A History of the Kings of England* (Leighton Buzzard, 1853)

Styles, P., *Studies in 17th century West Midland history* (Birmingham, 1974)

Thorn, F. and C., *Domesday Book: Vol. 16, Worcestershire* (Chichester, 1982)

Walker, R. O., *Hartlebury: A Record of a Parish* (Hartlebury, 1987)

West, J., *Village Records* (London, 1962)

West, J., *Town Records* (Chichester, 1983)

Willis, L. J., *Cambridge County Geographies: Worcestershire* (1911)

Willis-Bund, J. W., *The Civil War in Worcestershire* (Worcester, 1904)

Worcestershire County Council, *Worcestershire Countryside Treasures* (Worcester, 1973)

Index

131